Edward Octavus Flagg

Poems, Second Edition

And Later Poems

Edward Octavus Flagg

Poems, Second Edition
And Later Poems

ISBN/EAN: 9783744708913

Printed in Europe, USA, Canada, Australia, Japan

Cover: Foto ©Thomas Meinert / pixelio.de

More available books at **www.hansebooks.com**

POEMS

SECOND EDITION, AND

LATER POEMS

BY

EDWARD OCTAVUS FLAGG

NEW-YORK

THOMAS WHITTAKER

2 AND 3 BIBLE HOUSE

1895

THE DE VINNE PRESS.

Dedication

To my Departed Friends.

These lines ye may not scan,
Friends in the world immortal;
I give them by a plan
Of sweet compulsion
In Memory of Days ere ye had
    reached Death's Portal.

REV. EDWARD OCTAVUS FLAGG, D. D.

POET OF THE 52D ANNUAL CONVENTION OF THE
ALPHA DELTA PHI FRATERNITY.

DR. FLAGG was born at Georgetown, S. C., December 13, 1824. His father was Henry Collins Flagg, Jr., of Yale, Class of 1812; and his grandfather, Henry Collins, was surgeon in the Revolutionary army on General Nathanael Greene's staff. While at Yale, Henry Collins Flagg, Jr., a native of Charleston, S. C., met his wife, Miss Martha Whiting, daughter of Wm. J. Whiting, a court officer and a Yale man.

The subject of this sketch attended the Lancasterian school of New Haven, where he was the gold medallist as best scholar, and it was said of him by his teacher, Mr. John E. Lovell, that " he was able to do more things and do them better" than any boy that ever came under his tuition. His versatility was always remarkable. At thirteen he was offered $400 per annum as an assistant in a prominent school. After finishing a course of instruction at the Lancasterian and Hopkins Grammar School, New Haven, he studied civil engineering. He then entered Trinity College, Hartford. Among the first in his class while there, he was obliged, in consequence of financial depression, to leave before graduating. He studied law during a short period for educational training. Possessing a talent for music, he became a member of the choir of Trinity

Church, New Haven. Under the ministration of Rev. Dr. Harry Croswell, his thoughts were led to the study of divinity, and he became a candidate for Holy Orders. He pursued a course of theology under the direction of the Rev. Drs. Croswell, Cook, and Pitkin. Upon entering the ministry, his first charge was that of assistant to Rev. Dr. William F. Morgan (afterward of St. Thomas's Church, New York city) in Norwich, Conn.

An organization of a second church in that parish, called Trinity, resulted in his election to the rectorship. A fine congregation grew up under his pastorate, and another church was founded and developed in Yantic, Conn.

Thereafter he was associate rector of St. Paul's at Baltimore, Md., acting rector of Trinity at New Orleans, refusing the permanent rectorship at $6000 a year, and effectively recommending as his successor Bishop Leonidas Polk. He was rector of St. Paul's, at Paterson, N. J. After a year abroad for his health, he accepted a call to All Saints, in New York city. At the request of a few friends he organized the Church of the Resurrection, New York, which was eventually handed over to another presbyter. Again going abroad in consequence of ill health, on his return he supplied several parishes, including St. Mark's, in New York, where his ministrations were highly acceptable. He was long an assistant at Grace Church, New York, under Bishop Henry C. Potter and Dr. Wm. R. Huntington, where his powers of elocution were widely acknowledged.

His last charge was St. Mark's, Tarrytown, the rectory of which was purchased during his incumbency. Threatened with a second attack of pneumonia, he relinquished regular parish work.

Dr. Flagg came naturally by his abilities. His father was for five years editor of a Connecticut journal, and five years mayor of New Haven, as well as judge of the city court. He was a brilliant orator, and noted for his elocutionary powers.

The son's travels have been very extensive. While in New Orleans he was spoken of for bishop of Texas. It is said that while preaching in New York, his name, among forty-seven candidates, came before the council of the New York University as worthy the degree of D. D. Hon. James T. Brady, who had then recently heard of an extempore address of Dr. Flagg under embarrassing circumstances, warmly championed him, backed by Gov. John T. Hoffman, and of the three degrees then conferred his was one.

While preaching in New York, he was made chaplain of the Prince of Orange Lodge of Free Masons, and of the 9th Regiment of the N. G. S. N. Y. He preached at Col. James Fiske's burial; also a sermon over those who fell in the riots of '71. This was published by the press throughout the country, and was much commended for its eloquence and fearlessness, many congratulatory letters being received. During the visit of the 9th Regiment to Boston at the celebration of the Battle of Bunker Hill, he preached a patriotic sermon in the Boston Theater.

Colonel Fiske told his private secretary that his purpose was to erect for the Doctor ultimately as handsome a church as could be found in the city of New York.

Dr. Flagg has lectured extensively in New York, Massachusetts, Connecticut, and New Jersey, in schools and on public occasions. His lectures have been on history, logic, literature, and the English language. From early youth he has been a favorite of the Muse, and his love for versification has resulted in a large number of poems, most of which are the product of his later years. All of them show not only a musical spirit, but a decided originality and versatility. Among the most noted are " Live it Down," "Adirondack Poems," " A Word," and the Convention poem before the Alpha Delta Phi, in 1884, which fraternity he joined while in Trinity, and where he is often a toast-master among the Alpha Delts.

Flagg's poems have appeared in prominent journals in the East and middle West. Many have been set to music by S. P. Warren, Harrison Millard, and other composers. He published a volume including " The Prodigal Son," which won golden opinions. He is widely known as preacher, lecturer, and poet.

Dr. Flagg's first wife, Eliza W., was the daughter of Gen. William Gibbs McNeil, U. S. A., who was a graduate of West Point, standing at the head of his class. His second wife, Mary Lætitia, is the daughter of Judge Joshua Beal Ferris, late of Stamford, Conn., who was a graduate of Yale.

Dr. Flagg is a member of the Sons of the Revolution, Huguenot Society, the Ridgefield (Conn.) Club, and a number of other societies.

The American University Magazine.

PROLEGOMENA.

THERE is little allurement in our day to tempt the un-professional writer into the field of polite literature. The rewards of present fame or pecuniary profit are now reduced to a minimum — where they can be said to exist at all. As respects the verdict of posterity, however, another view offers itself. Certainly no harm is done in seeking it: for if the writing never reach the jury, literature will not suffer; while if it ever do get so far, it will be only because it deserves to be heard. Besides, he who writes honestly for posterity must be strongly impressed with the conviction that he has something particular to say; and the world is always the gainer by the work of an earnest man — unless perchance he be mad or silly.

It is a poor and contemptible lamentation of the un-successful writer, that there are already too many authors. To one holding such views, good sense ought to dictate that he would better quit the field, and not add to what he complains of as a nuisance. Unless an author thoroughly believes he has something new to say to the world,

> . . . there 's nothing so becomes a man
> As modest stillness and humility.

Yet I suppose the true reason why men write belles-lettres, in spite of the fact that publishers pay so few of

them for their work, is that many writers court a sympathy
for their thoughts they cannot hope otherwise to reach.
There is always a large number of men and women in
every community whose education and ideas are beyond
the appreciation of those immediately surrounding them.
They grow dissatisfied with the exercise of merely revolv-
ing their "thoughts, feelings, and fancies" in silence in
their own minds. It is a healthy relief to their mental con-
gestion when they have the courage to write them out.
Besides, by so formulating them, they can the better test
their coherency and soundness. Moreover, when once
written, they may be dismissed from the mind of the author, to make way for new ones based either upon, and
evolved from, what is thus laid aside, or upon what is
freshly originated from a new angle of vision. It was well
said, somewhat in this spirit, by La Bruyère: "When I
wish to forget anything entirely, I write it down."

But there is a great deal more than this. Every man
who really is inspired by the *mens divinior* has within him
what may be called a spiritual instinct for self-perpetua-
tion. He desires intellectual offspring. When he writes
with this aspiration, he spins from his own vitals as certainly as does the silk-worm. Coupled with this instinct,
when it is normal and sane, is the conviction that posterity
will "not willingly let die" his memory. So strong is this
overpowering faith that it often so overcomes his modesty
as to make him, like Horace and others, blurt out such ex-
pressions as *Non omnis moriar*, or *Exegi monumentum*, etc.
Who shall blame his honesty?

I have been led to these reflections by reading the foregoing biographical sketch of the Rev. Dr. Flagg, and examining some of the advance-sheets of a volume of his poems now in press. There are, in many of these verses, an impress of earnestness, a religious spirit, a fervor of patriotism, and a touch of deep feeling that need no apology for coming into the overcrowded mart of poetical offerings at this time. It is in evidence that a man who has led so busy a life was under the influence of some irrepressible *afflatus*, else he would have found occupation for all of his hours — when out of professional harness — without yielding to the importunities of the Muse. The brief verses "Live it Down" (often set to music), "A Word," and "Death is Swallowed up in Victory," to be found among the more recent poems in this collection, are specially to be commended to any susceptible reader.

From the touching verses entitled "A Word," a single stanza is here quoted as a specimen of the Doctor's musical quality:

> Perchance a word we now remember,
>   Of one long passed away;
> It comes back in our life's December,
>   A blossom of its May.
> Not volumes, with such gentle power,
>   The depths of soul awake;
> 'T will linger to our latest hour
>   For that loved sleeper's sake.

DECEMBER, 1894. A. M.

CONTENTS.

Contents.

Contents.

xvi   *Contents.*

THE PRODIGAL SON.

THE PRODIGAL SON.

I

HOME of old enchained the eye
    Of those its charms might see ;
Parental kindness wove a tie,
    From formal rule set free.
The wearied, there enticed to rest,
Could find some spell to soothe the breast.

II

In pride the brilliant lily grew,
    Which paled the monarch's sheen,
When gorgeous clad he met the view
    Of Sheba's noted queen.
Cool zephyrs fanned where fountains played,
And sweetest bird-notes filled the glade.

III

No careless wish, at random sent,
  Was ever breathed in vain,
And cunning skill, with kind intent,
  Stood near to baffle pain.
'T would seem one scarce could wish for more,
On earth, than blessed that home of yore.

IV

But strange, there dwells in wayward man
  A demon ill at ease,
Howe'er contrivance lays its plan,
  The changeful whim to please—
The word of fondness, winning smile,
Can ne'er from purpose rash beguile.

V

An elder son, severe and sage,
  Endued with self-control,
Sought first to nurse a father's age,
  And never wished to stroll
From scenes, wherein, his childhood reared,
The ripening hours had more endeared.

VI

Like nestling, beating half-formed-wing,
  Assaying flight in vain,

His brother scorned joy's well-known spring,
  Forbidden fruits to gain.
Impatient, like a mastiff bound,
He filled the air with doleful sound.

VII

To sire indulgent thus he spake,
  In tone unfilial, rude:
" My portion give, and let me break
  From scenes in which long mewed.
'T is hard to bear restraint unmeet;
I wish a stirring world to greet."

VIII

This heedless youth, with skill untried,
  Would tempt a stormy wave,
While those who oft have stemmed the tide
  Dare not such billow brave.
The early buds too soon will die,
And fledglings fall that strive to fly.

IX

Thus ever man insults that Will,
  Obeyed, revered above:
Yea, whispered accents mild and still,
  Embalmed in Jesus' love;
Distrustful as to daily bread,
Though like the sparrow, constant fed.

X

Since every effort proved but vain,
　To reach such truant mind,
The father, fraught with heartfelt pain
　That love had ceased to bind,
Though deeply moved his child to save,
The portion sought, reluctant gave.

XI

'T is thus, while leads that Shepherd's crook
　Which guides to pastures green,
Those deaf through sin, no longer brook
　A counsel wise, serene.
Permission tempts a soul awry,
Its own inventions crude to try.

XII

This younger brother sees a life
　Of pleasure, half-revealed,—
Those pastimes which with death are rife,
　Whose poison lies concealed,—
A thoughtless boy let loose from school,
Deriding all restrictive rule.

XIII

Endowed with means to suit his ends,
　Inconstant fancy please,

His mind perverted, close he bends,
　The shortest route to seize,
By which to gain the perfumed heights,
Where sweet Hymettus yields delights.

XIV

He would some " far off country " seek,
　Unvexed by precepts sage,
Where healthful warnings should not preach,
　From lips of hoary age.
He longed to roam in sunny lands,
'Mid mirth, and song, and sarabands.

XV

The sinner's haunts are far away
　From God's serene domain;
'Mid riot, pomp and roundelay,
　Where madness waits on pain,
Those Saturnalia, wild and deep,
In which both law and virtue sleep.

XVI

With lavish hand he strewed the wealth,
　His father kind bestowed.
He lightly ventured name and health,
　While free the goblet flowed.
The gold, long stored with frugal care,
Exhaled like mist that melts in air.

XVII

With forethought drugged, he tossed the dice,
  To artful rogues a prey :
In secret, where the gamester's vice
  Abhors the light of day.
By guile allowed, he won at first,
Till deep decoyed, he fared the worst.

XVIII

Attired in fashion's raiment new,
  Of costly fabrics made;
He oft appeared in varied hue,
  With silly dress parade.
By foppish trappings' tawdry glare,
He sought to make plebeians stare.

XIX

He roamed in halls of marble white,
  Enriched with bronze and gold,
Where windows flashing mingled light,
  Devices quaint unfold —
Gay nymphs and satyrs oft descried,
'Mid columns, bas-reliefs beside.

XX

Fair vases pleased, of Egypt's art,
  Surpassing later skill,

And Grecian taste performed its part,
  Some favored niche to fill;
The painter spread a wanton charm,
That gilded vice and augured harm.

XXI

The seas were dragged, the woods explored,
  Which dainty food supplied.
Choice wines, that clusters rich afford,
  Out flowed, a crimson tide.
Attendants grave, a dusky band,
Obeyed at once their lord's command.

XXII

In splendid chariot swift he rode,
  By prancing coursers drawn,
Equipped in latest courtly mode,
  They swept across the lawn —
Ambitious in his paltry lust,
To revel 'mid a cloud of dust.

XXIII

The syren Pleasure lured him on,
  To vilest haunts of crime,
Till shame had left its youthful throne,-
  That shield which guards our prime.
He sacrificed life's sacred hours
To Vice that haunts voluptuous bowers.

2

XXIV

A dulcet voice entranced his ear,
  Like chiming water's flow.
He deemed no lurking evil near,
  Presaging future woe.
As beauty spun her subtle thread,
Defeated resolution fled.

XXV

At game he lost, yet still he played,
  Until his hoard was gone.
His summer friends their exit made,
  And left him all alone.
A helpless wreck on fortune's main,
No beacon rose to cheer again.

XXVI

To drown remorse he quaffed the bowl,
  While imps shrieked through the air,
As reason fled beyond control,
  Uprose a lurid glare;
And when deep tolled the midnight bell,
Before him yawned avenging hell.

XXVII

By want distressed, he sought for aid,
  Of those his purse had shared,

But quick did summer friends evade
His suit — nor e'en had cared
Should he, so kind when they applied,
Through such ingratitude have died.

XXVIII

A mighty famine smote the land,
  Scant fruits the harvest bore.
'T was so when great Jehovah's hand
  Had Israel scourged of yore ;
When men despised those terms benign,
Declared by seer, upheld by sign:

XXIX

" A citizen " 't is told he found
  Amid his sorry plight,
Who soon to vilest service bound
  This man that scorned the right.
He sent him to the sty to feed
The unclean brute of sateless greed.

XXX

And could he, stricken thus, still rove,
  Yet longer leave his home ?
Despised and scorned, neglect that love,
  Whence madly lured to roam ?
Did Folly tread its thorny way,
Unblessed by Duty's filial ray ?

XXXI

So weak are all apart from God,
    Sad wanderers o'er the earth,
They lightly heed correction's rod,
    Impugn their heavenly birth.
But harder yet the lot in store,
For Crime will scourge them more and more.

XXXII

What thoughts within, conflicting burned,
    When pondering o'er his fate,—
To swineherd's menial labor turned,
    From rich and envied state!
Alas, the baneful fruits of sin!
Such prize do Pleasure's suitors win.

XXXIII

Can Jew descend to this gross task,
    Take charge of loathsome beast,
Whose flesh no hind would stoop to ask
    For meanest Hebrew feast?
Those demon-haunted go-betweens,
Where dwelt the heathen Gadarenes!

XXXIV

Behold a step beyond, Vice leads
    One duped through self-deceit.

Devouring hunger loudly pleads
  For husks the swine did eat.
But e'en such boon no hand would give,
That this poor famished wretch might live.

XXXV

No better lot mere Sense bestows,
  On such as woo her joys;
From worse to worse the victim goes,
  As Satan's art decoys.
Those bound to flesh who slight God's will,
With world husks ne'er can have their fill.

XXXVI

Now turn aside from this sad scene,
  With sacred lessons fraught;
In hope that all God's care may screen,
  From joys by ruin bought;
And let the heart its strength renew,
As brighter prospects meet the view.

XXXVII

'Neath yonder tall and beauteous tree,
  With branches spreading wide,
Inviting by its shade, to flee
  From heat and traffic's tide,—
Behold a feeble, outstretched form,—
A stranded bark in life's rude storm.

XXXVIII

He wears a garb of coarsest kind,
    His feet are bruised and bare,
The stifled, sighing, dirge-like wind
    Uplifts his silken hair.
Too soon the marks of age appear,
For Time could leave few tokens here.

XXXIX

His features, formed of classic mold,
    Were once a parent's pride;—
Misguided friends their beauty told,
    While worth was laid aside.
Indulgence, mark the fatal end
To which thy unsafe guidings tend!

XL

The tearful eyelids oft o'erflow,
    'Mid bursts of poignant grief,
As though the soul, oppressed with woe,
    Could never find relief.
A weeping child again we see,
In him abased beneath yon tree.

XLI

Reproaches come from every brute
    Which uncomplaining feeds,—

Content, enforced in language mute,
   With what supplies our needs;—
He learns how all God's creatures thrive,
Who by His law submissive live.

XLII

" Unto himself" he now has come,
   His manhood's nobler self.
A blessing sober thought has won,
   Transcending fame or pelf.
The grief he cannot longer bear
A bliss enfolds, which angels share.

XLIII

He muses, how the hireling bands,
   That serve his sire's full board,
Best food enjoy the yielding lands
   In harvest rich afford;
While famished he, with portion fled,
Could claim no place to rest his head.

XLIV

A late repentance melts his heart,
   And bends his stubborn will;
Deep yearnings, long repressed, upstart,
   Nor shame nor fear can chill.
They bid an injured parent seek,
So just and yet withal so meek.

XLV

" I will," the truant says, " arise,
   And to my father go.
Will say, ' My sin to heaven cries,
   A sin that brings thee woe.
Thy servant make me, call not son
An ingrate who such wrong hath done.' "

XLVI

A parent's love no tongue can tell,
   'T is like the ocean deep,
Which laves the shore with ceaseless swell,
   It cannot pause nor sleep.
'T is like the changeless stars above,
That never from their orbits move.

XLVII

Fit pattern He, who came to earth,
   From yon supernal home,
To save the lost of mortal birth,
   That fitful, foolish roam,—
With ardor chasing bubbles thin,
Which dance and lure to haunts of sin.

XLVIII

And ah, 't is oft the wandering child
   Towards which the parent leans;

Although to darkest deeds beguiled,
   This ne'er affection weans.
He sees, perchance, a fairer side
At times to reckless faults allied.

XLIX

Thus pause we o'er some statue old,
   Despite its broken grace,
Disfigured long by envious mold,
   On hand, on foot, on face,—
Which, yet a power of genius shows,
No common work can e'er disclose.

L

And so to Israel's bard of yore,
   Though stained with dreadful crime,
Jehovah tender feeling bore
   For David's love sublime.
His judgment Mercy soon effaced,
As this bright gem beneath he traced.

LI

Thus lenient he, in saddest mood,
   Whose son, long since away,
His father's counsel, sage, withstood,
   In distant lands to stray.
A void remained both dark and chill,
His brother strove in vain to fill.

LII

The gently sighing wind is fraught
  With eastern odors rare,
While many a gift is kindly brought
  To banish dull despair.
The father's spirit cannot rise;
A cloud obscures the radiant skies!

LIII

But now the son, with heart elate,
  His tears replaced by smiles,
Sets forth for home, with quickened gait,
  Surmounting weary miles.
As storm-tossed birds to covert fly,
This hapless youth did thither hie.

LIV

Thus hasten those by conscience pressed,
  Who grace once lost would win;
To seek again the slighted rest,
  And life anew begin.
They eager tread the narrow way,
Through many a gloomy, lengthened day.

LV

'Mid drear and rock-ribbed wastes he toiled,
  And frightening dangers braved,

His scanty garb was torn and soiled,
  While food he vainly craved.
His feeble limbs, his meager form,
Could scarce withstand the driving storm.

LVI

At each advance his nerve had failed,
  His strength had given o'er,
For fortune's blasts had oft assailed,
  And ills remained in store.
Yet Fancy sketched dear scenes beyond —
His soul could never quite despond.

LVII

His only bed the dismal ground,
  His roof the vault above;
His hardships so extreme he found,
  'Gainst desperate thoughts he strove.
But soon the light of opening day,
Restored fond trust with blessed ray.

LVIII

The *via dolorosa* One,
  With bleeding footstep trod,—
And he must choose that path alone,
  That seeks again his God;
If recreant e'er in noblest strife,
Which gains the font of endless life.

LIX

At last his native haunts are seen,
  As they were wont to charm;
Each well-known spot in memory green,
  Aloof from worldly harm.
Kind welcomes float from bird and rill,
With echoed strains 'mid glade and hill.

LX

Oh, most refreshing, blissful sight,
  In all this world of ours —
A gleam of once familiar light,
  From early cherished bowers;
When years have passed since youth essayed
To leave the home where childhood played.

LXI

And nought delights the vision more,—
  When long from fostering care
Of Christian nurture, heavenly lore,
  In sin's remorseless snare,—
Than light from that unshadowed clime,
Where seraph voices greetings chime.

LXII

And now, as mourning ewe perceives
  The lost returned from far,

While dingle, brake and shadowing leaves
  Her sense can ne'er debar,—
Through features changed, and plight forlorn,
The father knows his younger born.

LXIII

And as fond ewe, without delay,
  Leaps forth her lamb to meet,
No longer will that father stay,
  But hastes his son to greet.
He clasps and kisses once again,
The child who caused him anxious pain.

LXIV

Our condescending Parent kind,
  That light of every home,
The contrite soul will always find,
  Howe'er it choose to roam.
A pardoning kiss, a sweet embrace,
Will yet the chiding past efface.

LXV

The wanderer speaks, he pleads, " Forgive,
  Dear father, him who kneels,
A culprit base, unfit to live,
  And who just vengeance feels.
Thy servant make me, call not son,
A disobedient, faithless one."

LXVI

Observe how he o'erlooks the past,
　This soul oppressed relieves,
What guerdon binds repentance fast,
　How dear its blest reprieves!
No menial office will be given,
To one reclaimed from earth to heaven.

LXVII

He shall not wear those rags debased,
　A purple robe is brought,
A ring is on his finger placed,
　Of finest gold, well wrought.
His unprotected feet in shoes
No thorns can pierce, no stones will bruise.

LXVIII

The slave to freeman's state advanced,
　A robe and ring could claim.
Fit symbols these of lives enhanced
　From servile walks of shame;
When man by sin no longer bound,
Through faith released, in Christ is found.

LXIX

The fatted calf must leave his stall,
　To bleed for this event.

To boon companions one and all,
A summons far is sent.
" The dead now lives, the lost is found,
Oh, spread the glorious tidings round."

LXX

The happy parent cannot keep
Within his surcharged breast,
A pleasure fraught with import deep,
The homestead once more blest,—
But wide proclaims, his truant one
Is now again an honored son.

LXXI

As bidden guests are glad below
Through God's mysterious ways,
Most thrilling notes responsive flow
Where rise celestial lays;
Since e'en when one repentant sues,
Rejoicing angels bear the news.

LXXII

The tabret sends a merry sound,
The harp, the viol too,
The gleesome strains afar rebound,
Where smiles each sylvan view;
The long deserted chambers ring,
As friends elated dance and sing.

LXXIII

And where dwells he of cynic mold,
  Who chides such harmless mirth?
Does festal warmth a serpent cold
  In envy wake from earth?
No feast without its specter grim,
To dash the bowl e'er reached the brim.

LXXIV

As night steals on, the elder born
  Pursues his homeward way,
While mingling sounds not heard at morn,
  His eager footsteps stay.
He asks why orgies loud intrude,
To mock the evening solitude.

LXXV

Surprised he learns, quite safe and sound
  That brother long away,
Within his father's home now found,
  Awakens scenes so gay; —
The dance, the song, the shouts of glee,
From neighbors glad his face to see.

LXXVI

As flashes, 'thwart the cloudy sky,
  Precede a storm's descent,

So gathering gleams within his eye
Show anger's fierce intent.
He, unfraternal, will not come
To share his brother's joy at home.

LXXVII

But, like our Lord, persistent, kind
To those that mocked his name,
Who turned so oft the wayward mind
From stubborn, vengeful frame,
With mild entreaties seeks his sire,
To curb this restless, chafing ire.

LXXVIII

" For many years," declares the son,
" Thee faithful I have served,
Of thy commandments broken none,
From duty never swerved.
Yet e'en a kid has not been slain,
In proof that I thy rule sustain.

LXXIX

" But when, by many a harlot vile,
Thy gains have been devoured,
Upon a spendthrift thou dost smile,
And greetings fond are showered.
Though naught is done in my behalf,
For him is killed the fatted calf."

3

LXXX

The sire would such harsh thoughts allay,
  And motives just outline:
" Son, near me thou dost ever stay,
  And all I have is thine.
But now o'erjoyed we feast within,
Because a soul is saved from sin."

LXXXI

'T would seem the elder's sharp complaint
  Was urged by sense of right,
But different when the facts we paint
  Reflecting gospel light.
Broad truth disdains that narrow cell,
Wherein vain mortal judgments dwell.

LXXXII

The first-born brother,— stern and cold,
  Emotion kept at bay,
Imagined (cast in moral mold)
  His logic sure must sway,
Where one, to passion's spur a slave,
Had dared a parent's will to brave.

LXXXIII

He never felt the power of love
  To render service meet;

That found, the simplest act will move
  At gentle Mercy's feet.
Affection's aid he could not blend
With those their broken lives would mend.

LXXXIV

The Scribe, and Pharisee of old,
  Claimed pardon as a debt,
Their acts of merit loud were told,
  'Gainst each transgression set.
So sought the formal son to place
The law above God's boundless grace.

LXXXV

The father, like the gospel's Lord,
  While pleased with service strict,
To love would pardon swift accord,
  Though justice might conflict.
We thus discern free grace is shown,
That comes from God's eternal throne.

LXXXVI

Our story treats of ways divine,
  For all o'ercome with sin,
It doth a tender wish enshrine,
  The soul misled to win.
May matchless solace touch the deeps,
Where unconsoled repentance weeps.

LXXXVII

Lone child of frailty, long hath strayed
    In crime's unhallowed path?
By habit chained, art sore dismayed
    At black impending wrath?
Art crushed to earth, despised, forlorn,
No heart to rise 'mid social scorn?

LXXXVIII

Dost weep for sin's reproachful dye,
    For highest trust misused?
Doth waked contrition heave a sigh,
    For choicest friend abused?
Wouldst yet repair that shattered life,
So oft depressed with thickening strife?

LXXXIX

Then think of him in woful form,
    Who left pollution's mire.
He saw a bow above the storm,
    A patience naught could tire.
Repentance won a robe and ring,
Made happy neighbors dance and sing.

XC

Quick yield thy swineherd's wretched lot,
    And fly to sheltering home,

Where absent ones are ne'er forgot
By Him who bids us come.
A ring of freedom waits thee there,
A spotless robe thou too canst wear.

XCI

The merry heart of Christian thine,
  Beneath an ample roof,
No need of feast, of song, of wine,
  To aid Redemption's proof,—
But o'er thy brow a halo bright,
Will tell of changeless, pure delight.

XCII

Pray, never suffer evil eye,
  A brother's faults to view,
When purest saints, with thoughts on high,
  Indulgence humbly sue.
Without the Christ-atoning hand,
The test of justice none can stand.

XCIII

Thus He who treasured Mary's tears,
  Did Peter frail forgive,
Will quiet all tumultuous fears,
  Will cause the soul to live,—
Where faith and charity combined,
Rich fruits of hope shall ever find.

XCIV

And ah, corroding envy shun,
　When others win the race.
If they with footstep fleet outrun,
　'T were wise to mend the pace.
Unfair to grudge the better meed,
That well befits the better deed.

XCV

And view not with contracted look,
　This life — the Church — the State,
Each seeming difference mildly brook
　On God content to wait;
Convinced that He in future years
Will make more plain what dark appears.

XCVI

And ye who would improve mankind,
　Would point the better way,
Recall that father's constant mind,
　Unwearied by delay.
Let Love's inspiring flame still burn,
Although a son should not return!

ALPHA DELTA PHI POEMS.

ALPHA DELTA PHI POEM.

DELIVERED AT THE FIFTY-SECOND CONVENTION,
MIDDLETOWN, CONN., MAY 28, 1884.

I

FAIR city, which compos'd and queen-like sits
　　With vassal streamlet at thy side,
　Thy lovely picturesqueness well befits
　　These spirits choice, an academic tide —
Who lustrous by the gems of ancient thought,
To trace the beautiful have best been taught.

II

With love of learning and with open heart
　　Thy residents extend good cheer
To those for whom its living fountains start,
　　Who deem its rich rewards of mind more dear
Than ingots, which with pain are brought from far
Or trophies crimson'd with the gore of war.

III

Much pleas'd, thy sons and daughters do we greet
  For all invoking halcyon days;
May life's embittered cup be rendered sweet —
  Its gloom dispell'd by heavenly rays.
If corn and wine in other lands should fail,
May thy rich valleys ne'er such loss bewail.

IV

And as the muse, which lives beyond the age
  And smiles upon the time to come,—
May growing worth thy lengthen'd years engage
  And ratify thy nursing home
Of intellect, of prowess and of love,
Which from high truth immortal ne'er shall move.

V

A tender int'rest in our greeting wakes,
  As turn we to yon classic shrine,
Enlight'ning those for whose especial sakes
  These friends congenial now entwine,
And who of fellow-feeling touched the spring
Which from their daily cares old comrades bring.

VI

John Wesley, name to every Christian dear,
  Such monument was reared to thee —

Whom, if in world of light we may appear,
  Be sure we there with palm shall see
Well known among the beatific throng
That 'round the throne pour forth the seraph song.

VII

If undeserving, yet with pen aglow
  I speak for loftier name than all;
'T were well conceived that Wesleyan bestow
  On Trinity within her call,
The meed of clothing in poetic strains
Those deathless sentiments the soul contains.

VIII

Dear sister, on the wing of cherished love
  Accept our treasured memory kind;
We trust our hearts from thee will never rove
  Where leagues but few affections bind.
May health be theirs who mental tendrils train,
Thy chapter worthy ne'er receive a stain.

IX

And well it were we pass not coldly by
  The name of Berkley, prized so well,
And one long known to friendship's hallowed tie
  Whose precepts cannot fail to tell
When long forgotten is this favored day,
And o'er our sod the sighing breezes play.

X

Ye brethren of the Alpha Delta near
    Whom other institutions claim —
With unfeigned greetings we your hearts would cheer
    Whate'er may be your clime or name;
Accept a salutation fraught with power,
Whose bloom defies the bustling, fleeting hour.

XI

The motive which cements our cordial will
    Uprose from no mean, sordid bond —
Briarean are the welcomes we distil
    From choicest reminiscence fond;
Our Banian tree has planted wide and deep
From germs which were not born in cloistered sleep.

XII

We trust that all your cares are left behind,
    Beguiled by sweet communion's joy;
That blissful wakenings here you chance to find,
    Sad retrospect may not destroy;
And when enshrined within the heart of home
These scenes may linger, gladdening years to come.

XIII

But greeting o'er — to choose some fitting theme —
    A tribute meet where earnestness we find —

An undisputed duty plain must seem
Where thought is not to duty blind.
To *tendencies material* which appear,
In terms concise we would invite your ear.

I

Who dare assert our land is chained to sense,
To mammon-worship and to vain expense —
In what the wise esteem but toys,
Proud reason, deep-immersed in vapid joys —
That Darwin-like the masses seem to think
The chattering ape must be the missing link;
Or, Epicurus-like, the eternal soul
Base flesh did make and also doth control?
Sure lofty spires invite to realms above,
And pastors speak the words of heavenly love —
If ofttimes fearing it were not so well
To shock good taste with that proscribed word—*spell.*
Religion, perfumed, rises on the air,
While notes of sweet persuasion are not rare.
Then Education sheds her healthful smile,
With well-schooled measures seeking to beguile
From low, ensnaring and ill-timed pursuits,
Reducing to a level with the brutes.
Contrivances appear in every guise,
To lift the earth-bound to supernal skies,
To tear asunder from the mental gaze
Obstructions which conceal the truth's clear rays;

Yet still the carnal mind seeks carnal things,
Despite each plan which moral effort brings.
E'en as the cat which once was made a queen,
A mouse appearing still a cat did seem,
So those belonging to a sin-soiled race
For old enticements disavow their grace;
Professors grave and mitres, chair of state,
Become the same as at a prior date
Before transforming honor raised the wand,
Enabling to assume the higher stand.
An earthen vessel time at length reveals,
Although a precious treasure it conceals.

II

A moment let us glance the eye around
And trace such taint as in the Church is found.
The Church of Christ a spirit truth invests
As pure as snow-flake which on mountain rests;
A Bride of Spouse Divine she is proclaimed,
Of Him who in high heaven Chief is named;
Compared she is to that chaste silvery light
Whose effluence pure relieves the raven night;
She is to soar without polluting spot
In all the record of her endless lot.
But as 'mid Eden crept the wily foe —
Fair innocence ensnared with cunning low —
So coils and venomed slime are found within
That garden of redeemed ones, cleansed from sin.

Beyond the teachings of a simple creed
Corrosive fashion and vain rite proceed,
'Till Babylonian is the scarlet hue
That grieves the sober and reflecting view —
Or else, compounding with the natural man,
The Faith relaxes from her ancient plan,
And doctrine full of conservating power
Obeys the skeptic triumph of the hour.
The preacher's strength is on the human side;
Consulting taste, he must the Word divide;
Of vice in general he may speak at will;
Of vice particular, 't were best be still,
Else to his grief, and also his dismay,
He finds that he has preached himself away.
Religious entertainment men require,
And not for truth's sake they their clergy hire.

III

Then when we view Society, that state
Presumed upon religion to await,
Ordained for healthful purposes alone —
Supposed most rational in respective zone —
Much this is marred by horrid brazen crime,
More base than in the untaught early time
(Allowance made for heading of the press
That suits a morbid public — in the dress),
The mischief-loving sisters of Macbeth
May caldron stir, 'mid ceaseless dance of death,

Combining in their broth, some heads of banks,
With disunited couples from all ranks.
Alluding to a goodly, well-known state,
Where marriage banns did much on courts await,
A bishop once a distich did invent;
As memory serves, 't was somewhat thus it went:
" I say ' connect '— excuse the way 't is put —
When soon the well-feed lawyer says ' I cut.' "
Of yore, a chief position it is said
Was yielded to the heart and to the head.
But often now the heels usurp the place
Of intellect, the glory of the race.
To speak the German no one need assay;
To dance it, were the accepted better way.

IV

Grotesque the exhibitions that we see —
A comedy without th' admission fee.
Let 's take a peep at Folly's magic glass
And choose from modish figures as they pass.
Pray what is this that trips along the pave,
With arms akimbo and with visage grave,
O'erwrought in keeping one glass at the eye,
Resistive well-bleached collar rising high;
With curtailed overcoat and long-tailed frock,
And pantaloons so tense that children mock;
And bell-crowned beaver of such ample size
That vapory thoughts find space in which to rise;

With horizontal cane at midway held
As though each saucy poodle would be quelled —
That rashly questioned with a rival gaze,
This sample setting female hearts ablaze?
And what is this with wriggling, mincing pace,
Its hair descending o'er the nobler face,
With bonnet poised above the giddy head
As though of brains it had a dainty dread;
With struggling limbs in fettering silks encased,
With flying hands and lung-destroying waist,
Which seems a grasshopper of larger growth —
While to enlarge the mind alone seems loath?
Fantastic the conceit that thus would shine
Oblivious of an origin divine;
Why, pray, the painted savage more despise,
When so-called Christians don such queer disguise?
Of yore a pluck'd fowl Plato styled a man;
Perhaps such model serves a present plan.
Methinks less graceful is this hampered gait
Than that suggested by the unfeathered state.
Oh, when will Nature's face in charms appear
Of paint and dye relieved, and uncouth gear?

v

Note next the conversation of the day;—
How much in its behalf have we to say?
It gravitates upon the upper air
With which its thinnest gases may compare;

4

Not sparkling like the fluid in the glass,
Or glistening dew-drop crowning blade of grass,
With wit which, if not the highest, serves to cheer
And drive from grief's abode the rising tear;—
But seems it as to trees, mere oozing gum,
Or like on buoyant waters floating scum;
Unseasoned by the salt of healthful lore,
The man of thoughtfulness is styled a bore;
Instead of themes that lift the groveling mind,
The senseless and the child-like do we find;—
Or should the topic rise to serious grade,
It dwells on stocks, on market movements, trade,
Or last sensation in the journal read,
On those but lately married, or the dead.
Full many knit the brow in effort vain
To find out if to-morrow it will rain;
Or if 't is very hot or very cold—
Whate'er the weather — you will oft be told.—
But next — can conversation be enhanced
With thoughts so worthless in our books advanced?
Oft gravity is shocked with flimsy speech
Because of much that 's published in our reach.

I

Books to us are faithful blessings
    O'er the chequered path of life;
Soothing, full of kind caressings
    Are they 'mid this toilsome strife.

II

Yet are they as great an evil
When perverted from their end;
Children are they of the devil,
If foul error they defend.

III

Mental muscle fast increaseth
When with noble thoughts that teem;
Mental muscle fast decreaseth
If unreal as a dream.

IV

Trifling fiction much supplanteth
Fact, exalting, living, pure;
And the facile author granteth
What more purchases secure.

V

Books that read themselves are vended,
Which the sluggard mind enjoys;
And if crumbs of good be blended,
Sweet and vapid treacle cloys.

VI

Bacon, Locke and Aristotle,
Gibbon, Hume and Rollin, too,
Upstart authors quickly throttle —
An ignoble Waterloo.

VII

Light confections fail to nourish
  When the system strong meat craves;
So our minds cannot thus flourish,
  Sinking to dyspeptic graves.

VIII

And like books, so Art doth pander
  To a morbid, vicious need;
From its higher walks doth wander,
  Unenlighten'd tastes to feed.

IX

Classic schools are oft derided
  By the painters of the day;
Sordidly, it is decided,
  Classic schools will never pay.

X

Glittering and fantastic pictures
  Much the connoisseur offend —
Whereon artists place no strictures,
  Since the trade it doth befriend.

XI

Music and the art dramatic
  Bend low to the vulgar will,
While the critic — when emphatic —
  Doth with rage impostors fill.

XII

Poesy of noble mission,
  Sent from grossness vile to save,
Tell me, pray, what thy condition
  While sweeps on this vandal wave ?

XIII

Dost thou lift unsullied beauty
  Spite such devastation fell;
Hast forgot thy sacred duty —
  Errors' darkness to dispel ?

XIV

Shade of Shakespeare make thee stronger
  'Mid the slough of deep despond;
If thou struggle ages longer —
  Give to him thy fealty fond.

XV

Lo, the muse, with dastard yielding,
  Stoops unworthy crown to wear ;
Ne'er relenting, judgment shielding,
  Seeking soon such wreath to tear.

XVI

For the sake of favor winning,
  And the populace to please,
Oft we find the poet sinning
  On the side of pelf and ease.

XVII

Rhetoric takes the place of thinking,
    Luring with convenient haze;
Form, advanced with foppish prinking,
    Doth bewildered readers daze.

XVIII

Much the crowd affect to like it,
    Captured by a verbose show;
From the page would good sense strike it
    For one thought in lucid flow.

XIX

Note yon orb with frenzy rolling,
    While ascends poetic mist;—
'Mid vagarious numbers strolling,
    Vainly seek you for the gist.

XX

Milton vanish in confusion,
    Coleridge, Wordsworth, Pope and Burns:
Bleeding from severe contusion,
    Rest — neglected in your urns.

XXI

Turn we now from art and letters
    To the needful — judged by most;
Leaving verdict for our betters —
    To the criticising host.

XXII

Wealth our Father kindly gave us,
  In a soil of rare resource;
Much His aid we need to save us
  From a soul-consuming course.

XXIII

This a shining bubble dances,
  While the wise and foolish chase;
This the zest of life enhances,
  Spurs the slow, unwilling pace:

XXIV

Argonautic expeditions
  For the golden fleece equipped,
Rousing men in all positions,
  Eager rush they to be shipped.

XXV

Much of good the gold hath done us;
  Tears uprising doth it stay;
But, alas, it oft hath won us
  To forsake the better way.

XXVI

While the noblest are empowered
  With this tempting misused trust
Many fraught with virtue cowered,
  Soon are conquered by its lust.

XXVII

Oft it causes petrifaction
Where a Christian love should guide;
Oft foments a wild distraction,
Whence unnumber'd ills betide.

XXVIII

Social barriers are erected,
Shutting out the worthy poor,
Where, if merit were detected,
Wide would ope the bolted door.

XXIX

See entire nations bowing,
Dancing round the golden calf,
With their best the god endowing,
While complacent demons laugh.

XXX

Maidens bright, refined and comely,
In appeasement have been sold
To the witless, cross-grained, homely,
With deep pockets full of gold.

XXXI

Grammar tortured, port ungainly,
Do not lessen flattery's guile,
While good speech and bearing, vainly,
Seek to win approving smile.

XXXII

Little wonder — lured by money,
  Men will suffer, toil and cheat;
E'en as flies transfixed by honey
  They are held by this deceit.

I

As the sun golden
Rises at morning,
Nature adorning,
Sending his life-giving beam o'er the sea,
Bringing forth flowers,
Fragrant in bowers,
Grain in response whitening, covering the lea,
Sowing in harvestmen hopeful delight;—
So with full measure
Those tried with treasure
Freely should give,
Causing to live —
Cheering with slumbers kind,
Dark brooding night.

II

Oh, how we grovel
In palace and hovel,
Steeping the senses
In creature expenses;
'Mid dainties novel,

Reaping such fruits
As gluttonous brutes;
Eating the acorn, nor looking above,
Nurturing branches, feeding in love.

III

From dust we spring,
Of dust we sing,
To dust we cling,
Shrouding the beam of the undying soul;
Daily it pineth,
Droopeth, declineth,
O'erwhelmed by surgings that piteously roll.

IV

An age material,
Worldly, imperial,
Scouts as ethereal
    Chivalry's aims;
Eminent knowledge
Fetters the college
Life genial dashing,
As though 't were clashing
    With serious claims;
The secret society,
With badge of variety,
Reaching satiety,
Yields to propriety,

Clouding the festal ray
'Neath learning's dome;
The sweets of communion,
The service of union,
    Must vanish away
        Through edicts to come.

V

Again — we are so practical,
Exact and mathematical,
In business so fanatical,
    That forsooth
Some even would ignore
Or limit *classic lore*,
As bearing faint relation
    To the truth.
They would leave Olympic heights,
And extinguish ancient lights,
As but rubbish little suited
    To the need
Of a rising generation
Which must form the future nation
That should not any
    Lofty craving feed.
Thus the noblest thoughts that spring,
Which with inspiration ring
Uneffaced upon the brightest
    Page of time,

Are crippled by the fashions,
Nay, verdict of the passions,
And whatever is opposed to
   The sublime.

VI

Now, brethren, 't is your duty,
   Convened through social tie,
To strive lest low ambition
   Our heritage belie;
To yield to the material,
   Its fair, its proper place,
Resisting foul corruption —
   Its headlong, fatal pace;
To urge that coin be valued
   Alone for what 't is worth,
The same as occupation,
   Environment of birth;
Not made a god to worship —
   The lord of heaven and earth;
To banish all imposture
   Where'er its trail be found,
While treading with due caution
   Near consecrated ground;
To kindle love of country
   At shrine of love to man;
So pure in its devotion
   That angels e'en may scan;

To strive that chiefs like Pericles
  Be found to rule the State;
Or like the censor Cato,
  Aurelius, mild and great;
Or like the good King Alfred
  Who raised the Saxon race;
Or Washington, the peerless,
  Controlled by Christian grace;
To seek lest king-ruled strangers
  Who cast with us their lot—
Expose to foreign dangers
  Our Freedom's resting spot;
From brutal degradation
  To lift each sense-bound soul;
To aim, through education,
  The passions to control.
As in rude germ secreted,
  A plant may spring on high,
Unfolding leaves of beauty
  To greet the summer sky,
So most perverted manhood
  Conceals a plant divine,
Which with celestial glory
  Eternally may shine;
As Buonarotti's chisel
  An angel brought from stone,
So ye, to stainless being
  May lift the fallen one.

VII

As lifeboats in the storm
  Are launched upon the main
To cheer the sinking form
  With radiant hope again,
So men of Christian thought,
  While mammon's billows roll,
Your mission 't is to save
  From hapless doom the soul.
As o'er the treacherous deep
  The pilot keeps his eye,
Observe life's tempest track,
  Its ever-changing sky.
With wistful, tender care
  The pole-star guides at night;
So 'mid each doubt and fear
  Shines Bethlehem's watchful light.
Then seize the coming day,
  Its portents vast behold;
Whate'er the cost may prove,
  For God, for Right,— be bold.

FLORAL TRIBUTE TO A Δ Φ.

I

I SOUGHT the fragrant heliotrope,
  A gift, dear Alpha, loved, to thee;
For when the sun awakens hope
  His joyous beam she turns to see;
From him enticement ne'er allures,
  Unmoved by Art's or Nature's sway,
Her patient constancy endures
  When dismal shades conceal the day.

II

Our pride, our joy; thy spell we own
  Whate'er the charm that spreads its wiles,
'Mid every scene in every zone,
  From fond allegiance nought beguiles;
A sun thou art to lead us on
  With memories bright of genial mirth,
To bid unseemly care begone,
  And lend a glow to saddened earth.

III

Oh, modest make us like the hue
  Which decks the plain, unboastful flower;
For fragrant worth we also sue,
  A presence felt, a helpful power.

We trust, when leaves are scattered far,
And stems lie low before the wind,
The crescent proud, the radiant star
As loyal hearts again shall find.

WORK FOR LOVE AND DUTY.

I

WORK for love and duty,
    On thyself rely,
Crown with truth and beauty
    Alpha Delta Phi.
E'en the brightest morning
    Sheds a flickering ray,
Roseate hours adorning,
    Pluck the fleeting day.

REFRAIN.

Work for love and duty,
    On thyself rely,
Crown with truth and beauty
    Alpha Delta Phi.

II

Cease not star thy shining,
    O'er the crescent curve,
Growing, ne'er declining,
    Deathless hope preserve.

Towards each Mecca steering
  Brave to reach the strand,
Nought of danger fearing,
  Safe our bark shall land.
REFRAIN.—Work for love, etc.

III

Ne'er our zeal can falter
  Cheered by noblest aim,
While devotion's altar
  Glows with sacred flame.
Every brother drooping
  Loath to run the race
Humbly, gently stooping
  Urge his wearied pace.
REFRAIN.—Work for love, etc.

IV

May the vows uniting
  Pledged in days gone by,
Ne'er a comrade slighting,
  Sacred bind for aye;
While a world capricious
  Woos or turns aside,
Let no plot malicious
  Hearts endeared divide.
REFRAIN.—Work for love, etc.

5

V

Through the coming battle,
Plant the standard high,
'Mid the roar and rattle
Dare to do or die.
Sing the song fraternal,
Boon companions toast,
In the march eternal
Lead the living host.

REFRAIN.—Work for love, etc.

CHRISTMAS POEMS.

CHRISTMAS POEMS.

★

CHRISTMAS MEDITATIONS.

WHILE I sit musing this evening,
   Home scenes inspiring a song,
   Thoughts of my youth would I gather,
   Which to these visions belong.

Christmas is weaving its garlands,
   Sending its presents to cheer,
Lines of a brother I send thee
   Hallowed by memories dear.

Blest was the group of our childhood,
   Watched with its tenderest care,
When sorrow's cloud overshadowed
   Always an iris was there.

Bright were illusions, now broken,
    Precious the faces, now gone;
Fresh were the pleasures inviting
    Never in after years known.

Grand was the old-fashioned yule-log,
    Melting the frosts like the sun,
Or, like a kind nature beaming,—
    Welcomes withholding from none.

Icy winds scattered the snow-flakes,
    Shook the bare limbs of the trees;
Warm hearts with good cheer at Christmas,
    Arctic winds never could freeze.

Sympathy gave to the needy,—
    Those without fuel or food;
Outflowed a holiday bounty,
    Where it might do the most good.

Oft I recall those revered ones,
    Seeking the tendrils to train,
Whose words, like manna from heaven,
    Never shall reach us again.

Vivid that group seems this evening,
    Every bright face do I see;
Yet am I mocked by my senses,
    Most from their troubles are free.

May the sweet glamour, dear sister,
    Picturing days that are past,
Change to reality fadeless,
    Where such bright visions will last.

Gold is much valued of metals,
    Chiefly because it is rare ;
Home do we cherish more dearly,
    When fewer numbers are there.

Hence do we cling to each other,
    Even as wave clings to wave,
'Mid the long lost and forgotten,
    Each cherished link would we save.

CHRISTMAS CAROL.

HARK ! those strains, so sweetly falling,
    On that festal morn !
To our hearts are they recalling,
    Christ, our King, was born.
He has come to give a blessing
    To the poor, the sad ;
He has come with kind caressing
    Making children glad.

CHORUS.

Hark ! those strains so sweetly falling,
    On that festal morn !
To our hearts are they recalling,
    Christ, our King, was born.

Hie we to the lowly manger,
　At the village inn ;
Let us greet the wondrous stranger
　Saving all from sin ;
Let us bring a royal treasure,
　Like the wise of old ;
Love sincere and without measure,
　Better far than gold.
Chorus.— Hark, etc.

What though wintry winds are blowing
　Leaves from off the tree ;
And no more the flocks are lowing,
　On the upland lea ;
Christ each little lamb is tending,
　Folding it with care ;
From the storms of life defending,
　From its chilling air.
Chorus.— Hark, etc.

May those angels, at the dawning,
　Singing in the sky,
Ever with a kindly warning
　Bid the tempter fly.
When no more on earth is given
　Joy like this to-day,
May such messengers of Heaven
　Bear our souls away.
Chorus.— Hark, etc.

A CHRISTMAS CAROL.

WITHIN a stable cold and drear,
 The Lord of life is born ;
While lowly shepherds watching near
 Salute the Christmas morn ;
A light is shed to cheer the gloom,
 'T is not the sunbeam's ray ;
It shines to banish Sin's dark doom,
 As angels wake the day.

CHORUS.

Prolong, ye bells, the strain divine,
 Ye choirs, choice anthems sound ;
The fir tree bring, the laurel, pine —
 For Peace on earth is found.

O mother, watching o'er thy child,
 Enrolled among Christ's poor,
Thy burden cast on Jesus mild,
 And He will bless thy store ;
A Christ descends to free mankind,
 From each enslaving fear,
The careworn, needy, lost to find,
 And stay the falling tear.

CHORUS.— Prolong, etc.

Oh, boast not thou of gold and gems,
    Beyond thy fellows placed;
When He, supreme in loftiest realms,
    So mean a lot embraced;
The manger mocks vain mortal pride,
    Of station, wealth or birth,—
Exalts a Saviour crucified
    Above the thrones of earth.

CHORUS.— Prolong, etc.

And ye engrossed with self alone
    Of graceless frozen heart,
For past remissness quick atone,
    And of thy means impart;
" To live for others," glorious thought,
    The best by Bethlehem given,
In every Christian soul 't is wrought,
    It rules the Courts of Heaven.

CHORUS.— Prolong, etc.

TO A FRIEND
BORN ON CHRISTMAS DAY.

THE brightest day on earth
    Was that which gave thee birth.
Emmanuel was born
Upon thy natal morn;

Divine incarnate love
Descended from above.
With many thou art given
This richest boon of Heaven.
May joys with thee abide
Secured through Christmastide,
And grief stay but awhile
Dispersed by Jesus' smile.

ON VIEWING A PICTURE ENTITLED

" THE EMPTY STOCKING."

'TIS Christmas eve, with whistling wind
    And drifting snow and frozen stream,
While fancies weird excite the mind,
    And fireside joys more pleasant seem.

In yonder cot no contrast glows,
    To chase the gloom of Wintertide ;
No larder's store, nor ember shows,
    The picture smiles with winsome side.

A widow sits absorbed in grief,
    With Elsie nigh, a loving child ;
In vain she looks for some relief,
    As storm-fiends shriek 'mid orgies wild.

With tone assuring, Elsie's voice
  Suggests the coming Christmas morn;
Like all beside, would she rejoice
  To hail the day when Christ was born.

" Mama," she says, with fondest look,
  " My stocking must I hang this eve
In which I know some toy or book
  Good Santa Claus will surely leave."

The mother gives a glance of pain,
  As childish hopes are lifted high;
Without one wish to prove them vain
  She says, while 'scapes a mournful sigh,

" Your stocking do not hang to-night,
  Perchance you may not find it filled;"
She mused on their impoverished plight,
  With threadbare clothing, hungry, chilled.

" O yes, I must, I 've prayed to-day,
  Mama, you should no longer weep,
That Santa Claus would wipe away
  Your tears by gifts while fast asleep."

" God bless you for that prayer, my dear,"
  The widow says,— " I 'll ne'er repine,
But trust His word, nor longer fear,
  Though Christmas gifts should not be mine."

A spacious mansion full of light,
  Defies the raging storm without;
Profusely spread, exposed to sight,
  Are Christmas favors strewn about;

French dolls attired in silk and lace,
  That roll their eyes and even talk,
And dolls that move from place to place,
  By strange contrivance made to walk.

Choice albums bound in gold and calf,
  And Huyler's latest bonbons rare,
And monkeys stuffed that make you laugh,
  With greater beasts that make you stare.

Amid the group of various sort
  Are puzzles, games, and dancing-jacks;
Fierce soldiers that have never fought,
  And riders swarth on camels' backs.

But time would fail to mention all
  Arrayed to cheer the boys and girls,
From humming-top and bat and ball
  To mincing maids with bangs and curls.

A little one with soulful eyes,
  While nestled in her downy bed,
With earnest words her mother plies,
  Disclosing plans of heart and head.

She oft, it seems, across the street,
  The widow saw with daughter fair,
Whom always she would kindly greet,
  Though driven with a coach and pair.

Says she, " Mama, I hope and pray
  That Santa Claus will surely bring
Dear Elsie Brown, on Christmas day,
  Some useful and some pretty thing.

" The mother seems so very poor,
  And works so hard though wan and pale;
Just leave a present at the door,
  Lest Santa Claus should chance to fail."

The parent views with tender look
  Her child so pure, so full of love;
Reverting then to toy or book,
  Sure Elsie's prayer is heard above.

      .   .   .   .

Bright Christmas comes with cloudless sky,
  The earth is clad in bridal white;
While " Glory be to God on high,"
  Might well resound from height to height.

To seek her stocking Elsie goes,
  But finds it empty as when hung,
Her heart with sorrow overflows,
  By deepest disappointment wrung.

But lo, the cottage door she opes,
  And silken hose salute her eyes;
The contents seen awake new hopes,
  As charmed she stands in mute surprise.

A handsome purse with silver gleams,
  And dolls, with toys and sweets appear;
A book, with bright-hued pictures beams,
  And tales to suit the coming year.

An order in her mother's name,
  She then perceives,— to fill the hours
With work, for food and friendly flame,
  When cold the blasts and dead the flowers.

Each empty stocking God doth fill,
  If we His faithful children prove;
It only rests to do His will,
  To wait His time,— to look above.

TO A BEREAVED FRIEND.

HATH Christmas no bright wreaths for thee?
  Such woe is thine?
Why wilt thou with the cypress gloom
  Each thought entwine?
Not tears, but smiles become these days,
  Blithesome through Love.
The heart should echo songs of praise,

Swelling above.
Let Grief depart to Night's abode,
  With sable pall,
Since, in the East that Star arose
  Beaming for all.
The Lord, who with resistless word,
  Brought life at Nain,
Would rend the shroud that wraps thy soul,
  Raise joy again.
The blended notes that filled the sky,
  By angels given,
Proclaim — the dead in Christ are one —
  Household in Heaven.
The rarest flowers will often bloom,
  'Mid damp and shade,
From present sorrow blessings may
  Thy life pervade.
Oh, let the light of Christmastide,
  And the New Year,
Reveal the kindness hid beneath,
  Where frowns appear.

ADIRONDACK POEMS.

ADIRONDACK POEMS.

★

ST. HUBERT'S ISLE.

NUMBER ONE.

ID Adirondack beauty, Racquette Lake appears,
The fairest called, by some, of all the liquid chain ;
Its striking promontories, and its mountain views,
Its various windings, the surprises of its shores,
The smoothness, clearness of its water, when the winds
Allayed, refuse awhile to vex the elements,—
A picturesqueness give to fill a poet's dream.
On Racquette is an island scarce two acres broad,
The name is from St. Hubert, patron of the chase,
And well is it bestowed where choicest game abounds.
A church within its wood both grace and nature blend,
Near which are found the hemlock, pine, the spruce, and
  fern.
St. Hubert's jagged front, rude paths and rustic bridge,
Its scattered branches, rocks part clad in hoary moss,

The squirrel, reckless, freely bounding at its will,
The bird that fearless builds her nest, and pours her lay,—
Declare a spot remote, unfettered by the bands,
Enforcing mockeries — the bane of civil life.
This isle is fitly consecrated to its God.
This tenderloin of woodland doth Religion claim.
An altar has it framed, and rest for him who serves.
Protected is the shrine like that by Moses built;
Yet touch profane no dreadful statute here prevents,
But Reverence — assured through local metes and bounds.
Upon that holy day which sanctifies the seven,
If cloudless and serene the surface of the lake,
Like pinions moving, oars are plied the church to reach;
No vehicle with clatter shocks the air composed,
But, as by silent wing of angels, souls are borne
To where a common sentiment invites to kneel.
Within a leaf-girt harbor are the boats made fast,
Or, at a nearer landing lifted on a rock.
When ends the tolling of the bell that sweet resounds,
The voice of supplication and of praise is heard.
The preacher then, like John within the wilderness,
The truth proclaims, inspired by unseen presence felt.
When all have paid their homage to the forest's Lord,
On Him their burthens casting 'mid primeval works,—
The feeble and the strong, the hunter and the guide
To camp in view, or nestling down some bay, depart.
Then o'er the sacred island stillness reigns again,
Save where the sparrow chirrups or bee hums 'mid the
    flowers.

ST. HUBERT'S ISLE.

NUMBER TWO.

ON Racquette Lake, St. Hubert's Island
Arrests the eye — a lovely highland,
A noted feature in the skyland.
A church, with rectory is seen,
Inclosed by flower and evergreen,
A guide to point the wandering mind,
The regions of the soul to find.

The wave is oft with splendors glowing,
The majesty of sunset showing,
A richness o'er the landscape throwing.
The squirrel boldly climbs the tree,
The bird and butterfly soar free,
Protected near devotion's seat,—
From harmful snare,— a sure retreat.

Like doves unto their windows flying,
Note worshipers in boats outlying,
Who, toward the House of God are hieing.
The man of leisure and of wealth,
The invalid in search of health;
The huntsmen who 'mid deerland roam,
Now seek this consecrated Home.

The day is fading on the island,
The worshipers have left the highland,
Far down the lake or on the nighland.
Now vanished is the glare of day,
The moon asserts her gentle sway;
And seems with loving smile to bless,
This shrine within the wilderness.

SONG OF THE OPEN CAMP.

NUMBER ONE.

'TIS pleasant, after a weary tramp,
To meet at night in the open camp,
To feel the glow of the genial blaze,
That conquers gloom by its welcome rays.
We hear of many a trophy won,
By flood and field with the rod and gun;
The welkin rings with the song and jest,
Till sleep steals on and enforces rest.

The tie of friendship is always dear,
Let those it blesses be far or near,
A gem on shore or a pearl at sea,
A prize of age or of youthful glee,—
It gives content when all else hath flown,
Their names it hallows when friends have gone.
Not more on earth doth its charm inspire
Than when invoked by the camp and fire.

But few enjoyments we mortals know
With strange mosaic of weal and woe;
The blame for which may be ours or not
As each has used or abused his lot.
But zest is found that we ne'er forget —
A beam of hope ere the sun has set,—
It cheers by lake and by mountain spire,
In open camp with its social fire.

SONG OF THE OPEN CAMP.

NUMBER TWO.

LET jocund mirth beguile with song,
    The camp-fire burns to-night;
To us the sources true belong,
    Whence flows a pure delight.
That summer's dream will soon be o'er
    Is traced on flower and leaf,
Use well the moments yet in store
    Of earth's enjoyments brief.

Let Fancy weave to-morrow's sport,
    Of deer hunt, rod and reel,
Of base-ball and the tennis-court,
    Where wildwood odors steal;
But slighting not the guide boat's course,
    Through inlet, lake, and creek,
To where the rapids' noise and force,
    Dispute the point we seek.

Yet Wisdom's voice with loud demand,
Uncertain schemes would crush,
It much prefers the "bird in hand,
To two within the bush."
So ere the day, may each his part
Perform in blithesome mood,
Reproving every churlish heart,
That scorns a present good.

SONG OF THE OPEN CAMP.

NUMBER THREE.

U P the mountain,
    Towards the fountain,
Jubilant notes prolong;
    Earth rejoices,
    Distant voices
Echoing our camp-fire song.

Merry we carol to Hesperus far,
Drink to the moon from our cold-water bar
Fragrance of woodland alluring to stay,
Rivulet music inspiring our lay;
        CHORUS.—Up the mountain, etc.

        Proud emotion
        Like the ocean,
        Swelling and surging on,

Seems revealing
Nature's healing —
Life —'mid our pleasures won.

Free are our spirits from burthens released,
Freely we breathe — every muscle increased,
Fashion's restraints in these wilds are ne'er found,
Warbling of birds shuts out traffic's dull sound.

CHORUS.

'Mid the ringing
Of the singing
Guides draw near fire, to sate;
Flames are rising,
Night surprising,—
Love — thus o'ermasters hate.

Often we think of some others at home,
Fondly devising that hither they come,
Here at the open camp joining in sports,
Princes might covet as pastime for courts.

CHORUS.

THE BEAR IN THE ADIRONDACKS.

THE first bear I ever met in the Adirondacks,
Had such a paw
And such a jaw,
As did my courage sorely tax.

One day direct to Golden Beach
We rowed, and, when about to reach
    The strand,
    A figure dark,
    Upon a lark,
At frightened chickens rudely stared,
While, ogre-like, his eye-balls glared.

A lady in the boat who sat,
Quite anxious, queried, " What is that ?
    A dog ? " —
    " The critter there ?
    An old black bear," —
The guide said, resting on his oar ;
Her pulse leaped higher than before.

To youth, upon the land espied,
" A bear, a bear," the lady cried,
    " Run, run."
    Some Hectors flew,
    And shouted too ;
While panting for a gory fray,
They sought their arms without delay.

The uproar caused the bear to go,
But only with a movement slow
    And calm ;
    When out of sight
    The squad showed fight,

And made a Balaklava charge,—
But not too near the brute at large.

When speedily they all had fired,
Judiciously they all retired
      Unhurt.
      They shot, pray where ?
      Oh ! in the air;
These heroes wise, who came away,
Prepared to fight another day.

Advancing from his sure retreat,
The monster yet may chickens eat —
      And men.
      O lucky bear
      That was n't there !
Fair maidens o'er the warriors raved,
Who Bruin and themselves had saved.

MISCELLANEOUS.

MISCELLANEOUS.

★

ON THE DEATH OF LONGFELLOW.

DEVOTED watchers of the sky
    Upon a starry night,
Amid the orbs suspended high
    Exalt some favorite light,
Which, far beyond its fellows seems
Like Kohinoor, with peerless gleams.

But should they on some evening find
    That friend cannot be traced,—
An unseen hand where once it shined,
    Its glories had erased,—
No stellar beauty on its throne,
Could ever for this loss atone.

Amid the gifted few of song
　Whose treasures cheer our way,
A bard whom we have cherished long,
　Has calmly passed away.
No other genius owns his skill,
To charm the fancy, mold the will.

While wide the galaxy is fraught
　With those of radiant power,—
Who in the firmament of thought
　Will far survive the hour,
Amid the depth of present woe
Their numbers seem in vain to flow.

We mourn thee as the poet dear
　Who touched the simplest soul;
We mourn thee as one very near
　With purity thy goal.
The music of the " Psalm of Life,"
Renews each laggard in the strife.

Unnoticed Nature blooms beneath
　The magic of thy wand,
The tree, the flower, the shrub, the leaf,
　More beauteous deck the land.
Through thee, the very dullest sod
Seems fashioned by the hand of God.

The smith, the gleaner from the soil
  A common share may claim,
In thee, since thou to sacred toil
  Dost give its place and name,
Dost weave in verse a coronet
Upon its honest brow to set.

A field neglected thou hast tilled,
  And broadcast scattered grain;
We know from many a garner filled,
  Thou hast not sown in vain;
In distant countries fruits appear,
From seed which thou hast planted here.

At Pisa, in the spacious fane,
  The chord awaked below,
Arising, sounds in softer strain,
  Till lost in echoes low;—
So thy sweet thoughts will mount from time,
And mingle in the dome sublime.

A man in will, in faith a child,
  The children loved thee well;—
Allured by tones and bearing mild,
  They sought thy gentle spell;
Their innocence thy goodness saw,
By instinct's ne'er misleading law.

The home of Washington was thine,
  Whose valor won our State;
The Muse and Liberty combine
  To stem tyrannic hate.
A pilgrimage to such abode
Is prompted by a double goad.

His epic Homer gave to Greece,
  And Virgil sang for Rome,
And Shakespeare's strain will never cease
  To live in time to come;
But Longfellow will always be
The pride and glory of the free.

RENEWAL OF WORK ON THE PEDESTAL.

I

WHAT means yon stone?
  'T is promise vain of sculpture not completed.
    Alas, how lone!
No workmen seen; must Pride then be entreated?

II

'T is well thus far;
But wherefore, pray, the pile no more advances?
  What fickle star
To stupid sloth and base neglect entrances?

III

Hath fled the charm,
In Freedom's name, whereon our Hope was founded
To wrest this harm ?
Historic wraiths see stalk abroad confounded !

IV

Great Lafayette
And Rochambeau — the brave De Grasse — 'mid others —
In mute regret,
Would fan the flame this cold indifference smothers.

V

Alas ! how droops
The eagle's wing, beyond his eyrie soaring !
What dying swoops !—
Niagara's flood, meanwhile, a protest roaring.

VI

Renew the task —
A signal meet for every struggling nation —
Nor let them ask
If yet we bear to Freedom's cause relation.

VII

When faint the sense
That limned the Stars and Stripes our flag enfolding,
'T will glow intense —
The gift of France, in beauteous grace beholding.

VIII

Those hither bound
Will read a truth while here perchance they tarry;
When home is found,
The noble truth to other lands they 'll carry.

IX

Let each in love
Some tribute give,— a patriot's willing token,—
Faint hearts to move,
That far and wide the oppressor's chain be broken.

A HYPERCRITICAL WORLD.

PARAPHRASED FROM THE AFGHAN.

STRIVE as you may to gain the good opinion
    Of man, so hard to please;
And soon you 'll find, from king to lowest minion,
    On trifles most will seize,
By which to torture with malign inventions —
    To make your right seem wrong —
When naught but e'en the very best intentions
    To every act belong.

Let youth, within the snares of dissipation,
    Resolve the better way,
Constrained will be pronounced its reformation,
    Postponed till latest day.

A purpose grave, a manly resolution,
  Says Rumor, shares no part,
In what appears a moral revolution
  Affecting mind and heart.

If thou wouldst silent sit instead of prating,
  Whatever be the cause;
Some reason false, ingenious slander stating,
  Vaunts zeal for social laws.

The spirit of the coward is imputed,
  If thou dost weigh thy speech;
" 'T is plain," it says, " and ne'er can be refuted,
  The rogue would overreach."

Or, if thou art inclined to conversation,
  Of sentiment or wit,
Some self-styled critic of thy generation
  In judgment harsh will sit;—

Will say in undertone, with shrugs and winking,
  " No substance here is found,
This fluent phrase contains but little thinking,
  'T is all unmeaning sound."

If seclusion thou prefer,
  To the clamor and the stir,
Of an uncongenial crowd,—
  Men will call thee cold and proud.

If thou mingle with thy kind,
   To relieve of care the mind,
Some will say, " Yon lazy lout
   Is a worthless gad-about."

If a fortune one should gain,
   After years of toil and pain;
And he spend it on himself,—
   Men will say, " The stingy elf."

If one freely scatter gold,
   And his charities be told,
'T will be said, while some applaud,
   " He secured his means by fraud."

E'en the poor and honest man,
   Scorning every unfair plan,
Will be sneered at as a fool,
   Who observes the golden rule.

If one seem quite neat and nice,
   In the latest mode precise;
" A Miss Nancy," men will say,
   " Who in prinking spends the day."

Or, if one be plain in dress,
   Not on fashion laying stress,
A coarse sloven he'll be dubbed,
   And by snobs perchance be snubbed.

But let a carping world censorious prove,
　Should this, from what our conscience bids us move?
Not they to greatness soar who heed such scorn,
　From fools ejected and of envy born.
The Roman warrior, the Grecian sage,
　The saintly few whose lives redeemed their age,
'Mid floods of censure, vile as undeserved,
　A bearing brave, persistent have preserved.
Then let the crowd misjudge thee as it will,
　With sense of right, be firm, press onward still,
And as the eagle soars beyond the cloud,
　Looks down unmoved above the lessening crowd,
Far o'er the dwindling critics thou wilt sail,
　And smile at those whose schemes can naught avail.

INDIVIDUALITY.

NO two alike on earth are made,
　All differ, if by faintest shade;
Distinction marks created things,
From beast that prowls, to bird that sings;
The fish that swarm within the sea,
The insect tribe, from mite to bee,
Have diverse features deep inlaid.

Why thus should oneness be impressed,
On objects in resemblance dressed,
Except variety of sounds
In Nature's harmony abounds;

That self alone should be preserved,
Originality conserved,
Whereby we speak and act the best ?

Some often will a model take,
From chance acquaintances they make;
From cynosures who cause a stir,
Through gifts conferred on him or her;—
They think, e'en in their faults attired,
That they will be as much admired,
As those praised for their virtue's sake.

The protean man is now alone,
Next, normal self has quickly flown;
Behold him stately and erect,
Then see him smile and genuflect;
To-day he seems quite rational,
To-morrow, international,
With lisps and shrugs and foreign tone.

To-day he is æsthetical,
But this is hypothetical,
For, 'mid the changes found in life,
The cockney slang may soon be rife ;
His mother tongue receives a blow
By " thanks awfully," and " you know,"
More vulgar than poetical.

Alas, when wisdom stamps the age,
Doth imitation thus engage ;

The classic Romans aped the Greeks,
Disturbing Cato by their freaks;
The token we can scarcely find,
That tells the independent mind —
'Mid quest for what is " all the rage."

The rose courts not the lily's bloom,
.Nor envies she her sweet perfume;
But each in beauties given doth shine
Admired alike, from source divine;
No more should we our gifts despise,
On others look with envious eyes,
Unmeaningly their ways assume.

CALAMITY.

CALAMITY! Oh, whence dost come,
Thou grim destroyer, laying low
The good, the grand, the beautiful —
Ignoring treasure, haughty mien,
Triumphal arch or state of kings —
The gems of genius, wrought by Art,
The pride of cities — hope of man ?

Dost come through accident — caprice
Of great creation's potentate ?
In mercy to a suffering world,
With besom dost thou harsh approach —

That many more may grow and live,
In purer, higher walks, which lead
To summits of eternity.

Jehovah, who the lily gave,
The rose to bloom and cheer the way
By common footsteps trod — who lights
With central fire, diffusing warmth,
And opening nature to the eye —
Who night adorns with silvery orb,
'Mid changeless lamps of gentle beam,
Descends in flood and hurricane,
In bursting cloud and lurid glare,
In desolating famine, sword
And pestilence, with ruthless scythe —
To bless in ways we cannot see.

The forge of love, with glowing heat,
Of visitation, handling rude,
To stern endurance frames the soul,
Which brings at length to pastures green,
Whose margents waters still inclose.
Therefrom are wrought in spotless white
Kind ministries that never cease
Dispensing comforts, which engage,
Like visions of a holy eve —
The peaceful iris, mists disclose,
And resignation blinding tears.
A country wounded statesmen heal.

From war's defeat new heroes spring.
The smitten rock clear water yields.
To Moses, God, through fire, is known,
'T is only, after dread portents,
Elijah hears the still, small voice.
From depths of woe, yet unrevealed,
Come life and immortality.

TO BE A PROTESTANT.

TO be a Protestant is what ?
　　To be a man of narrow mind ?
Who hates all others of his kind ?
To charity, to reason blind ?

To be a Protestant is what ? —
To be a friend of liberty ;
To think the truth will make us free —
To hate and strive 'gainst tyranny.

To be a Protestant is what ?
To feel for all a Saviour died,
Low superstition to deride,
To read God's word whate'er betide.

To be a Protestant is what ?
To keep our country, as to-day,
Apart from foreign despots' sway —
To God, through Christ, alone to pray.

BE LOWLY, O CHRISTIAN !

I

BE lowly, O Christian, to all of thy kind,—
A brother despise not, impoverished, obscure,—
God sealed him thine equal, with heart and with mind,—
Not less for his rescue did Jesus endure.
By deed as by word let the poor man believe
Thy vows to thy Master, ne'er made to deceive.

II

Pray how art thou better than penury's child,
With station, subservience to wealth at command?
Durst vaunt of a nature than his less defiled,
A soul more defended from sorrow's dread hand?
Alike may ye taste of life's bitterest draught
Sin's chalice commingled by both may be quaffed.

III

The nursling of fortune, inflated with pride,
Surrenders conceit to the dust of which made,
E'en Tarquin Superbus must sleep side by side
With sycophant vassal of commonest grade.
The despot who governs a world by his nod,
Ignoble must die at the mandate of God.

IV

A signet divine wears the humblest brow,
A coronet bright above rags may be seen;

A fair pearl of Grace may the plainest endow,
  A soul unpolluted 'mongst hovels is clean;
No atom of gold would you cast to the wind—
Some gold in each mortal, observant, we find.

V

Be lowly, then, Christian, nor let worldly caste
  Wear haughty demeanor to those of one birth;
Let toil-worn, neglected feel Christ's love is vast
  Through those who proclaim themselves followers upon
Thus concord may reconcile differing estate   [earth.
Till Labor on Capital patiently wait.

THOUGHTS ON VISITING THE GRAVE OF GENERAL ULYSSES S. GRANT.

I

TREAD softly by the river,
  No common relics lie
Beneath yon mound, which seems to say,
  "The great, the good must die."

II

Tread lightly by the river;
  Ye see no tyrant's grave—
Who trampled on the rights of man—
  Beside the peaceful wave.

III

One sleeps whose courage failed not
'Mid war's most maddening din,
Yet gentle as the gentlest child
That slumbers free from sin.

IV

When blackest clouds hung o'er us
In dread fraternal strife,
A chieftain new revived the hosts
And raised from death to life.

V

No tempest rose more direful
Abreast the ship of state.
The sturdy pilot grasped the helm
Deciding human fate.

VI

" If needs," said he, " all summer through
On this line I will fight."
Such iron purpose cleaved the way
To Richmond's distant height.

VII

His name can never perish
Who gave the Union birth;
And green his wreath will ever be
Who slavery swept from earth.

VIII

And while we laud the manhood
　That dealt the patriot blow,
Our hearts commend the christian love
　Which raised a fallen foe.

IX

So long as beauteous sunset
　Shall glow on Hudson's tide,
Will live the tale how blue and gray
　Wept, standing side by side.

X

That " mercy shown to others "
　He cannot fail to find,—
Eclipsing far the dazzling fame
　The soldier leaves behind.

THE HIDDEN CROSS.

SCARCE ever to the eye appears,
　The cross within a soul's domain,
'T is bathed in silent, secret tears
Therewith are blended unknown fears,
　A muffled grief, an untold pain.

Perhaps it is a broken vow,
　A faithful loving heart betrayed;

The wreath torn from a hero's brow,
Before a rival weak to bow ;
  A wound by hollow friendship made.

Anon it is the wear and tear
  Of active life, of toil for bread,
Dependent little ones in care ;
Perchance a pauper's grave to share —
  A hopeless weeping for the dead.

Whate'er it be of heart or mind,
  Or anguish caused this nerve-strung frame,
In every child of woe we find
A cross to which the world is blind —
  To rich, to poor, to all the same.

Would we this unveiled sadness heal
  And stay the deep dark Marah-tide ?
Another cross doth Christ reveal,
Which all of grief cannot conceal
  Where Calvary's streams of mercy glide.

THE BREAKER.

A TINY fleck of purest white creeps on from far,—
  Apace it comes with growing form,
And now 't is lost, as lost in clouds the trembling star,—
Again it speaks the hastening storm.

Anon, as sensitive and deep stirred swells the breast,
It rises stately towards its height
Till dashed against resistful rocks in wild unrest,
Its form is soon removed from sight.

While many tearful eyes perceive the distant foam;
Upon the face dismay is told;
A watery winding sheet it seems to hearts o'ercome;
The ardent pulse of youth grows cold.

Though wrecks, with loved and lost, the treacherous
 depths bestrew,
Who cheerful bounded o'er the main,
What heeds the mocking breaker gathering force anew,
Presaging tempest fierce again?

While o'er the misty way we float towards spirit clime
Some breaker rises, sure if slow,
The faithful soul defies the ruthless floods of time,
As yon stanch cliff the rage below.

THE BELL BUOY.

A BELFRY on the deep;
 No land appears,—
Yet mystic chiming strangely fills the air,—
 It wakes from sleep,
 It conjures fears,
 The source,—pray where?

Thou buoy that floats the wave,
The secret tell —
" Unwary ones that heed not dangerous shoals "—
These notes would save;
My seeming spell,—
" The sea controls."

'Mid dancing, thoughtless spray
These sentry sounds
Betoken grief for those who sleep below,
A dirge-like sway
From ocean mounds —
An echoed woe.

Within each human breast
The soul to keep,
A warning bell to every one is known;
.   This signal blessed
Mocks self-willed sleep —
In undertone.

'T is not on virtue's tide
Its sounds we hear,
But when sin's treacherous waters, seeming fair,
Their perils hide —
In kindness near —
It rings,—" Beware."

ON THE DEATH OF NATHANIEL SMITH
RICHARDSON, D. D.

H E fell with his armor girded on,
Equipped for the thickening strife;
The prize, through the Master bravely won,
At once crowned his useful life.

He valued the truth and sold it not,
Did benison come, or blame,
A message from God he ne'er forgot,
Spite interest and scorn the same.

While purblind prophets gave ready ear,
As syrens their world-strain sang,
Disdaining all sordid, craven fear,
His tocsin unceasing rang.

He watched with care, lest the Church, the Bride,
From Bridegroom should be divorced;—
While fiercely brake the opposing tide,
Of Christ, the Head, he discoursed.

Repose in peace with each loyal heart,
The palm of the Just be thine;
Thy choice was the hard but better part,
Upheld by a voice divine.

Whoe'er may condemn thy conscience word,
  Can scarcely fail to admire
That spirit in man which will be heard,
  Undaunted by sword or fire.

May those commissioned by One on high,
  Be ever as leal as he;
In love may they all as faithful vie,
  That Sion from taint be free.

For place or pelf may they not be found,
  Accepting the false, if new;
In doctrine may each be stanch and sound,
  If kindred souls be the few.

VAIN REGRETS.

WHO that looks upon the past
    Does not ponder?
Who that reads its strange neglects,
    Does not wonder
If the coming days shall prove
    Any better?
Whether Haste or Sloth shall write
    Such dark letter? —
Waste no sighs on what can ne'er
    Be prevented,
Acts to which a pliant will
    Hath consented.

Careless seedsmen oft become
   Far more chary,
If the birds devour the grain
   When unwary.
Dost thou for thy planting lost,
   Trouble borrow?
Prayerful sow, and thou shalt reap
   Joy, not sorrow.

THE SILENT MARCH.

THE march of life is onward ever,
   Its fleeing moments spurn delay;
As soon may man from being sever,
   As cease to tread its solemn way.

When least aware we still are moving,
   All pilgrims toward an unseen goal;
If slothful, or our days improving,
   We float along as billows roll.

Nay, e'en when Sleep asserts dominion,
   Earth slumb'ring 'neath her drowsy reign,
The swift-winged Hours ne'er fold a pinion —
   Their flight no less though star-beams wane.

We cannot change the tide when flowing;
   We cannot bind the zephyr free;
We cannot breast the life's on-going,
   Like streamlet gliding toward the sea.

Momentous this resistless marching,
　　This silent step toward shores unknown —
'Mid Alpine glacier, desert parching —
　　Its footprints found in every zone.

But, oh, to ponder mystic winding
　　In realms beyond our vision's range!
That paths there trod we here are finding,
　　Is theme for musing, wondrous strange.

THE TOMB OF JOSEPH RODMAN DRAKE.

A SIDE from traffic, in a humble brake,
　　Repose the relics of the poet Drake ;
No classic column with surmounting bust,
　　As yet denotes where lies the silent dust ;
But willows lowly o'er him weeping bend,
　　Dejected by the loss of Nature's friend.
Although the Muse bewailed him in his prime,
　　And Halleck grieved at Death's untoward time,
Yet thoughts of ripeness and of Living Truth
　　Adorned the treasures of a well spent youth.
The " Culprit Fay," a pure aerial sprite,
　　And " Freedom's Flag " with hues of heavenly light ;
And " Gentle Bronx," whose unpretending tide,
　　Doth through his magic numbers sweetly glide,—
Are deep inlaid upon the scroll of fame,
　　The deathless record of a well earned name.

Though lightly did the bard esteem his worth,
  Consigned at last to this secluded earth ; —
The fragrant wild-flower blooming near his bed,
  The wind that sighs, from briny billows shed,
The lark that breaks the loneliness of morn,
  The harvest ripening with its wealth of corn,
Seem now to speak, prophetic of that hour,
  When Drake in bronze shall test the artist's power,
When merit shall its due award receive,
  And Genius slighted need no longer grieve.

ODE TO STATEN ISLAND.

AN isle with lovely shore
    O'erspread with rural bloom ;
A city vast before
    Enwrapt in misty gloom.
This pleasant isle,
Not many a mile
    From where men pant for room.

What place more fair conceived
    In Fancy's realms of light,
Which those from toil relieved
    May greet with favored sight
At set of sun,
When work is done,
    And slow descends the night ?

At Kill von Kull a ray
  In beauty decks the sea,
At close of sultry day,
  When fettered limbs are free.
A picture — joy,
The heart's decoy,
  Bids brooding sorrow flee.

But yet, ere eyes grow dim
  To note the passing year,
These gardens, neat and trim,
  Perhaps will disappear,
Till urban shade
Shall shroud the glade,
  To please coarse traffic's whim.

But let the prophet tell
  How landmarks are removed,
I'll ne'er defy the spell
  Of present objects loved:—
The bird and tree,
The humming bee,
  Resistless charms have proved.

Mosquitoes, Standard Oil,
  Or more unpleasant things,
Shall try in vain to spoil,—
  I mind not fumes nor stings.
A rural smile,
Enchanting wile,
  Their fond oblivion brings.

TAKE NO THOUGHT FOR THE MORROW.

W E eat the bread of care;
    From morn to night we toil,
Ne'er free from anxious thought,
Begrimed with mundane soil.
We climb as though for life;
On summits would be placed;
We build vast futile plans
By time to be effaced;
Absorbed in self alone
Man envies those who rise;
Let struggling victims groan
He seeks to snatch the prize;
He vaunts and hugs his store
As though 't were all in all,
False laurels would he wear
Though dearest friend should fall.
His country or his town,
His party house or name,
He writes with glowing pride
And blends them with his fame.
Poor dupe of vain ambition,
He ne'er has wisdom found,
His grasping disposition
Shows heart and mind unsound.

. . . .

A chieftain from the forest

Who lived from day to day,
As thrives the cared-for sparrow
Or beast that finds its prey;
Who slept on grassy pillow
Content with Nature's fare,
With humblest comrade willing
His fortune rude to share;
Is brought to greet a city
Where art's attractions rise,
Where palaces and towers
And parks salute his eyes.—
His guide, supposing, dazzled
At sights so rare as these,
The wild and dusky savage,
Asks what his taste might please.
The chieftain, nought affected,—
As deems his eager host —
Doth ne'er vouchsafe to mention
What charm delights him most;
But lost in grave reflection,
This strange response doth give,—
" It seems to me you white folk
Try very hard to live."

LIFE IN DEATH.

(A group of passengers on a sinking ship join hands and perish
together.)

O UT on the sea,
Far from the land,
Buoyant with glee,
Floats a gay band.

Hope's banners fly,
Laughter is loud;
O'er heart, o'er sky,
Hovers no cloud.

Out on the sea,
Far from the land,
Hushed is the glee;
Storm waves command.

Soon on the deep,
Dangers appal:
Death's final sleep
Waiting for all.

Out on the sea,
Far from the land,
Souls shall be free,
Hand clasping hand.

Singing a hymn,
   Breathing a prayer,
Sense becomes dim;
   One grave they share.

Tossed on the sea,—
   Safe on the shore,—
Christ's should we be,
   One evermore.

Happy such tie,
   Sealed with last breath,
Witnessed on high,
   Hallowing death.

FIRST IN PEACE, FIRST IN WAR, FIRST IN THE HEARTS OF HIS COUNTRYMEN.

I

FULL tribute pay to him who, first in peace,
Demands that grateful tokens never cease.
The earliest helmsman to our bark of state,
In civic power uprose a leader great.
Wild faction's storm his skill at once allayed,
Who governed self and thus the people swayed.
The olive twine for him, our birthright won—
Our heaven-ruled President — our Washington.

II

He, first in peace, as first in war, we place,
When on the field his martial course we trace.
'Gainst soldiers, battle-trained, he drew his sword,
Inspiring untried troops with cheering word.
But human rights his willing footsteps led,
And thus he conquered while dissuasion fled.
The laurel weave for work so nobly done,
In freedom's cause, by valiant Washington.

III

Each distant land resounding echo gives
That first within his country's heart he lives,
A patriot true, awake to duty's claim,
His honor dearer held than wealth or fame.—
At last, when all his lustrous traits we scan,
Our judgment yields approval to — a man.
With amaranthine bloom that braves the sun,
Let memory crown the peerless Washington.

WINTER.

BOISTEROUS winter, prophet of ill,
Rough side of nature, desolate, chill,
Killing the flower, stripping the tree,
Forcing the song-bird southward to flee,
Driving the kine from bleak field to stall,
Heaping the snowdrift over the wall,

Rifling of verdure grass-laden mead,
Sealing in earth the slumbering seed,
Hasting the twelvemonth sere to its close,
Numbing the muse that genially flows,
Sporting at will with shivering forms,
Filling with dread at gathering storms,
Slippery pavements, tottering gait,
Causing delay, till keen frosts abate.
Winter enchaining the body and will,
Swift stream arresting, hushing the mill,
Heedless of murmurs heard from the poor,
Hungry and half-clad, found at the door.
Messenger dread, congealing the breath,
Curdling the blood, and warning of death —
Hie thee far hence, thou grim Arctic shade,
Get thee where sunbeams never pervade.
Ungracious winter, harsh dost thou seem,
When disenchanting autumn's soft dream.
Yet if we judge in kindlier mood,
Candor reveals a friend true and good;
Rough in demeanor, tender in heart,
Such is the verdict time doth impart.
Often seems fortune dismal at first,
Clouds of destruction ready to burst,
While underlying mercies divine
Shine like the gold relieving the mine;
So with thee, winter, deemed most severe,
Favor diffused, will surely appear.
Rosy-hued health is borne on thy wing,
Pestilent fever no more is king;

Over the slothful thy bracing sway
Banishes languor, seizing the day;
Home made the stronghold, decked with more
    charms,
Terrors external wholly disarms;
Thine is glad Christmas, yule-logs aglow,
Evergreens torn from fast clinging snow;
And though some mourner drop a sad tear,
Spirits elate salute thy New Year.
Thine merry sleigh-bells, rush of gay steed,
Coasting, lithe skaters graceful in speed;
Thine the glad moonlight, glittering star,
Flashing Aurora shooting afar;
Pendants adorning roof-top and tree,
Branches in mail which flash like the sea.
Hard-favored winter spread like a pall,
Heaven-favored winter smiling on all.

LIFE AS IT IS.

THIS life is but a thing of fears,
    A dream of hopes, of smiles, of tears —
A blossom which at morning blows,
A blossom which at evening goes —
A flower tinged with beauty's blush,
Which any thoughtless tread may crush;
A sky of azure, fair and bright,
That storm-clouds quick obscure from sight;

A moonbeam's evanescent play,
Which ere the day-dawn speeds away;
A bubble floating on a lake
That soon a passing breeze may break;
A wave which tosses high and free,
Then dies upon a tranquil sea.
Life as it is — a songster proud
Which leaves its perch to seek the cloud,
But soon falls low with flutt'ring wing,
No more to soar, no more to sing.
Oh, fearful art thou, human life,
Thou fitful thing, thou thing of strife!
Why mock us with the promise bright,
Then leave behind the gloom of night?
Not so that life which is to be —
There no alloy, no mockery,
No transient smile, no bitter tear,
No intermingling hope and fear;
No fading light, no short-lived bloom,
No preparation for the tomb;
No palsied joy, no fleeting breath,
No throbbing pulses, hushed in death;
But as the eagle soars from sight,
And leaves behind each mountain height,
Ne'er pausing in his upward way,
While yet remains one golden ray,
So soars man's spirit, once set free
In that pure life which is to be.

IN MEMORY OF THE LATE REV. STEPHEN H. TYNG, D. D.

I

NOT every hero guards the eternal cause —
　　A beacon light:
On Zion's heaven-lit towers the warders pause,—
　　Nay, yield the fight.

II

It brightens hope to trace — where softness reigns —
　　Unflinching nerve;
The valiant few who offer self, time, pains,
　　Their King to serve.

III

One hence has gone, with iron purpose fraught,
　　To speak as told
From Sinai's mount, or where the Saviour taught
　　In words of gold.

IV

His matchless trust he did not vend at will —
　　A huckster vile —
To changing markets in celestial wares
　　Of any style.

9

V

One central truth enlisted thought and breath,
　　'T was Jesus' love;
Discoursing how it brought up Life from Death,
　　He sought to move.

VI

Crowds pressed to hear, because he held the Cross
　　In open view;
Like Paul, he deemed all else on earth but loss —
　　Such mind they knew.

VII

As shined to Constantine the signal weird
　　By which to win,
There seemed before his daily sight, upreared,
　　This cure for sin.

VIII

Socratic power informed his ripened speech,
　　Instructing youth;
Unmoved by threat or favor, " apt to teach "
　　Fair Wisdom's truth.

IX

Take heart, ye timid guides, who fear to tell
　　The " narrow way ";
Let soldiers brave, in Christ who war so well,
　　The spirit sway.

I LOOK BEYOND.

I LOOK beyond this teasing care,
  Which, like the stinging pest,
  That will not let me rest,
    Drives reason from her lofty throne,
'Mid hopeless, grim despair.

I look beyond colossal wrong,
  With shameless Gorgon head,
  A timid nation's dread,
    Which makes an oft-defeated will
To cringe before the strong.

I look beyond the lessening light,
  That surely, slowly fades
  'Mid gathering evening shades,
    While breathings weird from mystic realms
Reveal 't will soon be night.

I look beyond the thoughts that craze
  The weakling, finite mind,
  That sees not God behind,—
    Whereby this perfect plan doth seem
A wildering needless maze.

Ye troubled children of to-day,
  Whose hearts are in a sphere

We know must disappear,
    Pause not to dream and moan and pine,
But look beyond, I say.

TO BESSIE, MY ELDER DAUGHTER,

ON HER SIXTEENTH BIRTHDAY.

JUST sweet sixteen—that golden age,
    Enrolled on life's mysterious page,
When, childhood's hours of sunshine gone,
Some cherished hopes have with them flown.
Dear Bessie, 't is a parent's will
A child thou shouldst continue still;
That freshness yet suffuse thy heart,
And true nobility impart;
That guilelessness may never cease,
But always cause thee inward peace;
That youthful trust may gently twine
Its fadeless wreath of love divine,
Whose pensive halo on thy brow
May ever seal the fontal vow;
That thou submit to His kind hand
Who points us to the better land.
Be simple in thy every aim
And heed not fashion's hollow claim.
If others seek in wealth to shine,
Let household virtues pure be thine.

Remember, beauty e'en most rare
Without discretion is a glare,
And duty should our time employ,
While pleasure is a wayside toy.
Obtain the precious wealth of soul
Whose winning and whose strong control
Will charm when youth has had its day
And human graces lose their sway.
That God may bless thy future years
And give thee more of smiles than tears,
And thou at last His joy may share,
Dear Bessie, is a father's prayer.

TO SALLIE, MY YOUNGER DAUGHTER,

ON HER SIXTEENTH BIRTHDAY.

BEYOND the river Acheron, in Greece, it was supposed
That classic gardens in their bloom the asphodel
exposed,—
This faithful flower place near thy heart, which constancy
will teach;
Such emblem for thy life on earth — a future life will reach.

The jassamine, of spotless white, with leaves of brightest
green,
Is known, by fragrance sweet exhaled, before its form is
seen;

It breathes of kind pervasiveness that fills a loving face;—
Let friends at distance know thee near, through pure
affection's grace.

The humble broom a monarch plucks to deck his royal
crest;
This modest plant with dignity did valiant knights invest;
So let thy unpretending worth suggest a purpose higher,
To meet the choice of Christ our King, thy first, thy last
desire.

BEAUTIFUL HUDSON.

O BEAUTIFUL Hudson, roll on in thy might,
So wooingly bathed in the moon's soft'ned light!
How fain would I watch from the highlands above
Each bark on thy breast, like a snowy wing'd dove.

Most pleasant to ponder the Catskill's repose,
As deepens the shade at the day's gentle close;
To linger in summer time near Tappan Zee,
'Mid song of the wood bird or hum of the bee!

O beautiful Hudson, thou stream of my heart,
Awakening thoughts that can never depart,
How sweet to recall on the far distant strand,
Thee, fairest of rivers that grace our free land!

Let other bards sing of the beautiful Rhine,
Whose turret-crowned hills bear resemblance to thine,

But give me that stream which on Nature alone
Has builded her claims and established her throne.

THE AIR OF SIASCONSET.

THE air of Siasconset,
  Is fortified with health;
'T is full of benediction,
It yields far more than wealth.
It turns despondency to joy,
And man becomes again—a boy.

It lifts the soul to heaven,
Whence every good descends,
It banishes ill feeling,
The genial mind befriends.
Malaria—hated poison—flies,
Its ills to plant 'neath other skies.

When wearied in the city,
O'ercome with heat and toil,
We sigh to tread the paths once more,
Upon this wave-washed soil,—
To breathe where Sanketty's head-light,
Dispels the sailors' fears at night.

The wild rose we would gather,
That decks Nantucket isle,

Would revel in its fragrance,
And catch again its smile;—
Would sip the tonic Neptune gives
By which the drooping spirit lives.

Of elements protected,
From touch of aught unclean;
In laboratory faultless,
Whose workings are unseen—
Is formed supply of best ozone,
To wand of science ever known.

Grotesque is Siasconset,
With relics strange and old;
Yet they who seek to find them,
Attractions more behold;
But chiefly are we bidden there,
By power embosomed in its air.

CAST ANCHOR.

TWO vessels start upon the deep
    To reach a distant shore;
'Mid storm-winds rising from their sleep,
    And distant storm-waves roar.

"Cast anchor," speaks a solemn voice,
    'T is madness to proceed;

One captain makes a fatal choice,
The other quick takes heed.

Ere long the wild o'ermastering gale
Ingulfs a reckless crew;
While safely rides a folded sail
Above the waters blue.

Two youths start forth upon the tide
Of life's uncertain sea;
"Cast anchor" on the heav'nly side,
Speaks forth Eternity.

For one that voice is raised in vain,
The other marks its notes;
A human bark is driven amain,
Its fellow safely floats.

Seems all above serene and clear
Within this world of ours?
Behold yon darkling cloud appear,
Which o'er the sunshine lowers.

"Cast anchor," friend, within the veil,
And let wild billows beat;
They cannot o'er thy faith prevail,
Disturb thy sure retreat.

ON HEARING THE EVENING GUN AT QUARANTINE, STATEN ISLAND.

HARK to the sound of the evening gun,
Proclaiming the work of day is done;
Dismissing the sons of toil to rest,   .
While drooping the bird now seeks its nest.

Hark to the sound of the evening gun,
It speaks of the hour when hearts are won,
When Cupid shall weave his mystic spell,
Which on the unending years shall tell.

Hark to the sound of the evening gun,
It bids us observe the setting sun,—
That, with its last ray, the dreams depart,
Which brightened at morn the sanguine heart.

Hark to its cheerful tone, "All is well,"
As dying upon the ocean swell;
It loudly declares—One never sleeps,
Who tender and faithful vigil keeps.

Hark to the sound of the evening gun,
Reminding of evil we should shun;
It asks "Till to-morrow, why delay—
A summons of duty's voice to-day?"

Hark to the sound of the evening gun,
It warns us the race is nearly run,
It echoes, " The strife will soon be o'er,"
While booming along the distant shore.

MY FLOWERS.

A Dying Mother's Request to Her Daughter.

COME closer to thy mother dear,
   And place thy hand in mine,
I feel the warning very near
   When earth I must resign.

One simple charge to thee I make,
   Which charge, if thou obey,
Content I 'll let the angels take
   My spirit far away.

The boon I ask is — that these flowers,
   Which, 'mid the wintry gloom,
As though just washed by summer showers,
   Send forth their sweet perfume,

May be the objects of thy care,
   As they have been of mine;
That thou 'lt protect each leaflet rare
   Nor let their beauties pine.

Observe them e'en as I have done,
  With ever anxious eye,
Be wary lest a single one
  Untimely droop and die.

And think not that the boon I crave
  Ill-suited to this hour,—
That 'mid delirium I rave
  About a transient flower.

I 've watched each rosebud slowly ope,
  I 've seen each lily fade,
With one my soul renewed its hope,
  Which with the last decayed.

These silent teachers sweetly tell
  The story of Christ's love,
Vain doubts depart as by a spell,
  Where words could never move.

Oh, may our Father by such means,
  Exalt thy soul from earth;
While on His strength thy weakness leans,
  Who gave these flow'rets birth.

DEDICATION OF AN ALBUM

Belonging to a little girl celebrated for her musical talent.

FAIR child, this world is now but new to thee,
While hope paints what the coming life may be,—
But trust not hope, for oft she hath deceived
The young, who have her promises believed.
Yet should thy future days be dark or bright,
Thy wounds a balm may find, thy footsteps light.
Obey the guidance of our Friend on high,
Who leads to where the verdant pastures lie,
And thus life's roses shall expand for thee,
While thou its thorns shall never feel nor see.
Improve thy gifts and cultivate the heart,
And blessings shall be thine where'er thou art.
Thy guardians will approve, esteem will grow,
The streams of self-respect unceasing flow.
God grant thee power long to sing and play,
And chase from many an eye the tear away,
Till, at the last, a mystic harp be given,
Whose thrilling tones thy skill shall wake in Heaven.

THE MAGDALEN'S PRAYER.

DEAR Saviour fold me in thy love,
And take me to thy care:
From intercession's heights above,
Oh, hear a sinner's prayer!

A scornful world derides my tears
   And casts me from its sight;
Let thy free pardon quench my tears,
   With all-prevailing might.

The lab'rer seeks at eve his home,
   With footstep light and free;
But I from morn to night must roam,
   Bow'd down with misery.

Alas, a thoughtless hour beguiled
   Amid the paths of shame —
I deemed him true who falsely smiled,
   To rob me of my name.

As now I gaze on yonder tide,
   With waters dark and deep —
My foul disgrace I fain would hide
   In death's oblivious sleep.

But yet I shudder as the winds
   Seem searching to my heart; —
A hidden power my purpose binds,
   And from myself I start.

Dear Saviour, thou dost intervene,
   Restraining my intent —
Thy watchful mercy now is seen
   This madness to prevent.

The fallen sister thou didst raise
  And soothe her throbbing breast,—
And should I fail thy love to praise,
  And on thy word to rest?

Then, Jesus, fold me in that love,
  And take me to thy care;
From intercession's heights above
  Oh, hear a sinner's prayer!

PARTING HYMN AT THE VAN NORMAN INSTITUTE.

Written for the Class of 1879.

MINGLED emotions, engaging the heart,
Sadly remind us that classmates must part;
Leaving the dreamland of girlhood's fresh life,
Seeking the upland in earth's fitful strife.

Lasting are ties which so tenderly bind,
Comrades engrossed in the treasures of mind;—
While union, springing from fancy, must wane,
Ours deeply rooted will ever remain.

May the good seed with such carefulness sown,
Yield when the days of our youth have long flown;
In the hereafter, when mortals are free,
Glorious fruitage may all of us see.

Teachers so patient and schoolmates so dear,
Mem'ry will hallow through each changing year.
Ever be vivid those fast speeding hours,
Which we have shared amid learning's fair bowers.

Blessings for all who, assembled to-day,
Wish us God-speed on the uncertain way;
May they with reverence always thus prize
Knowledge, that legacy sent from the skies.

Help us, kind Father, our duty to know,
Led by Thy hand,—in its path may we go;
Feeling that guidance, protection and love,
Never will fail where our aim is above.

ATHEISM.

WE here were placed to perish like the brute,-
Though sorrow has our portion been,
And hope has ne'er fruition seen,—
Forever must the lips in death be mute.

The invalid with languid pulse and eye,
The laborer bending 'neath his care,
Who must his daily burdens bear,
Sees at the end no prospect but—to die.

He, long immured from light, with clanking chain,
　　The man of every friend bereft,
　　Without a face of kindred left,
Must look beyond conjecture's mists,—in vain.

As they who cast their nets and nothing found,
　　When gloom of night did long invest,
　　And weary limbs obtained no rest,
Are we with life-work buried in the ground.

No promise comes the final hour to cheer,
　　When racking pains disturbed repose,
　　And weeping friends predict the close,
And next await the knell, the shroud, the bier.

Such cheerless view, perverted science takes;
　　She tells us, this poor life is all,
　　The future hiding with a pall,
That, when man dies, he never more awakes.

Assumption most fallacious, most unwise,
　　It makes Creation but a joke,
　　And Providence dissolves in smoke ;
Our planet seems a mere balloon that flies.

No stimulus exists for hero's deeds,
　　For truth's advance, mind's higher play,—
　　But honors merely of a day,
While partially are given this world's meeds.

10

Much we prefer to place before such dross,
  Some signal of a land in store,
  Some sunbeam from the Evermore,
Some vision of the all-prevailing Cross.

To lift the soul, so oft obscured by tears,
  To give a purpose and an aim,
  For love disclosed to each the same ;—
We need some Revelation through the years.

And when, at last, in Time's relentless date,
  We reach the problem of the sod, ˉ
  'T were well to feel " there is a God,"
And yield to Him the spirit and its fate.

ON SEEING A PICTURE OF HOMEWARD

LABORERS AT PRAYER.

DEVOTION'S hour is drawing near,
  Yon little chapel lifts its spire ;
All work is o'er and now appear
  Those seeking home in soiled attire.

As slow the evening shadows fall
  And mellowed beauty fills the sky,
A heavenly light descends on all,
  Who grateful kneel to One on high.

God bless the workmen of our land,
  And make them cheerful 'mid their lot;
And may a smiling Christian band
  Be found in every humble cot.

THE WINDS.

YE winds speak a language consoling or sad,
  As trifling through arbors, or seemingly mad;
While cooling this evening my o'erheated brow,
Ye tell of some streamlet with cadences low.
Like dirges ye sound from the old Abbey walls,
Or castle historic with desolate halls.
When shrieking at midnight, with terror ye fill,
As though ye were laden with tidings of ill.
Ye storm-winds that dismally howl o'er the deep,
Seem mourning for loved ones the loving must weep.
Ye mutter, O north winds, of ice-fettered lands,
Restraining the frolicsome wave with your bands,
As death puts to silence a child's harmless glee
Ere echo respond to its laughter so free.
Yet kind are your words to the heat-stricken soil,
Dispelling the languor from wearisome toil.
Ah, welcome Zephyrus, from yon favored clime
Where Poesie's triumphs mock old Father Time,
While chilled are our spirits by pitiless frost,
Proclaim to us visions of loveliness lost.
When erst to Eolus Ulysses had come,
By thee was he gently brought back to his throne;

So summon the Ithaca fair that we knew,
Ere faded the scenes of our childhood from view :
Let tones early treasured again greet the ear,
Oft lending a smile which would vanquish a tear.
Let once more the mocking-bird thrill with his lay,
Reminding of happiness, not long to stay,
The oriole bring with its beautiful hue,
Which glows like the heart of a Southerner true,
Inviting the stranger to tarry and share
His board, though supplied with the commonest fare.
The voice of the south wind speaks peace to my soul,
A life, I disclose not, its accents control,
With kindness that leads me to more pensive hours,
When soothingly floating 'mid gardens of flowers.
It sweetly retraces fresh days that were mine,
Where grow the magnolia, the orange and vine.

ON PRESENTING A FLORAL HORSESHOE
TO A BRIDE.

GOOD luck be thine,—
May love entwine
Its garlands for thy life;
May iron heel
Ne'er crush thy weal,
In guise of wedded strife.

As fades each flower
In every bower,
So beauty droops its head ;—
'Neath love's control,
Peace fills the soul
When youthful charms have fled.

NEVER DESPAIR.

NEVER despair, if afar, unalluring,
    The heights to be scaled ere the shadows descend;
Let courage be instant, thy footstep assuring,
    While hope, the kind handmaiden, smiles to befriend.

Never despair, if when livelihood seeking,
    Or honest repute in profession or trade,
Misfortune with direful purposes reeking,
    Thy life-earnings scatter, thy just aims invade.

Never despair, if when bravely contending
    For freedom, for all that is dear to the soul,
O'ercome is the castle of truth while defending,
    The cohorts of Belial wresting control.

Never despair, if the church or the nation
    Surrender to ignorance, interest or fear,
If progress expire in a wide desolation
    And Dagon and Bel in each temple appear.

Never despair, if thy good should be doubted,
　Thy toil for the welfare of others be blamed,
Thy efforts for conscience be sneeringly scouted,
　And selfish, deceitful, thy mission be named.

Never despair, if the blight of some illness
　Should wither the dreamland of unfading joy,
If pain, never ceasing, monotonous stillness,
　Through wearisome watchings thy peace should
　　destroy.

Never despair, if thy pulse be declining,
　The sands of existence fast passing away,
When, too late, the season for useless repining,
　The spirit is leaving its prison of clay.

Never despair, if thy burden seem greater
　Than man can endure in his sensitive mold,
And take not, but cherish that life the Creator
　Bestowed for some end His wise counsels enfold.

Comfort descends from hope's fetterless regions,
　From martyrs in glory through echoing air,
Attested by throngs of beatified legions—
　To fainting hearts whispering—Never despair.

ON THE NEW VERSION OF THE SCRIPTURES.

OH, give me back the old words,
  The words to memory dear,
I do not like the new words,
  They harshly greet the ear ;
I love the words my mother taught,
  In voice of mildest tone,
As borne by swift-winged seraphs,
  They went up to the throne.

Oh, give me back the old words,
  In school-room heard of yore,
Before instruction's round began
  In varied tasks of lore ;—
A solace when the book was read
  Within the house of prayer,
When pointed out the strait gate,
  And shown each sinful snare.

Oh, give me back the old words
  Oft uttered on the wave,
When, 'mid the storm's commotion,
  I felt but One could save ;
My eyelids could not close at night
  Without both shame and fear,
Unless I read those verses,
  Profound and yet so clear.

Oh, give me back the loved words,
  Which soothed the aching brow,
When all of earth's prescriptions
  No healing could bestow ;
Upon the weary couch they cheered
  When filled with racking pain ;
'Mid cruel disappointment,
  When life seemed dark and vain.

Ere dust to dust be spoken
  Above the gloomy sod,
And upward soars my spirit,
  To reach the realms of God ;
I do not wish a different phrase,
  From that oft heard before,
As through the aisle so hallowed
  Some cherished form they bore.

If creed be known through language,
  And who can say 't is not,
Then should those well-known symbols
  Forever be forgot ?
They still convey the buoyant thought
  Of angels near the throne,
The light to mortals given,
  Oppressed, o'ercome, alone.

It may be that the new words
  Can please the scholar-mind,

But in the old revered ones
    The saving truth I find.
For me their simple Saxon ring,
    Their quaint and homely power,
Exceed by far in sweetness,
    This fashion of the hour.

NO NORTH, NO SOUTH.

FROM loving lakes that seaward flow
    To golden mines of Mexico,
From Eastern mart to Western coast
'T is now a freeman's honest boast —
        No North, no South.

The wounds are healed that brothers made
From Maine to tropic everglade;
All cold suspicions now have fled,
Are with vindictive embers dead.
        No North, no South.

The chain in which the slave was bound
Clanks not with harsh unchristian sound;
False zeal provoking latent strife
No longer seeks to jeopard life.
        No North, no South.

A heavenly voice has hushed to peace
Where warring words might never cease,

By raising those within our land
Long years restrained through party's band.
        No North, no South.

God keeps His children low in dust,
To purge away their cankering lust,—
Then kindly lifts to joy again
When wrong succumbs to healthful pain.
        No North, no South.

Avaunt ye lingering ghouls of hate,
Be emulous to raise the State;
Revive not more the checkered past,
On Lethe's wave dead issues cast.
        No North, no South.

An hundred years have fled away,
The Country stronger day by day,
For 't is not man that gives us life,
But One who stills convulsive strife.
        No North, no South.

And speed the cry—no East, no West,—
No foreign sway—nor worst nor best—
With specious wiles shall clog the stream
Of progress towards the Nation's dream.
        No North, no South.

REFINEMENT.

FROM God is given a human frame
  To intellect allied,—
And means by which to mold the same,
  His providence supplied.
He chief performs creation's will
  Who treats his gifts aright,
Who makes them all their parts fulfill
  Till growing to their height.
When stern utility has wrought,
  Refinement claims a place,
And ceaseless toils till powers are fraught,
  With skillfulness and grace.
Thus man like some strong building seems,
  Enduring and adorned,
Or like a beauteous ship whose beams
  And hull for strength are formed.
Or like some landscape bold and smooth,
  With rock and lake and sky,
Which speaking use and beauty soothe
  And gratify the eye:
He needs not wealth to give him place,
  Or favor of the great:
He shines an honor to his race,
  With neither gold nor state.

EASTER CAROL.

I

BEAUTEOUS Easter morn,
　Roseate beam of love,
Brighten, bless, adorn,
　Smile from realms above.
Modest opening flower,
　Fragrant greets the sky ;
Lift us by thy power,
　Vows ascending high !

CHORUS.

Beauteous Easter morn,
　Roseate beam of love,
Brighten, bless, adorn,
　Smile from realms above.

II

Grant relief to care,
　Cause alarms to cease,
Broken lives repair,
　Paint the bow of peace,
Let each bond be rent,
　Envy bid depart,
Give the poor content,
　Move the churlish heart.

III

Shine 'mid household gloom
Ne'er dispelled before,
Let Emmanuel's bloom
Crown each pagan shore:
Till forgiving ray
Gleam above the rod,
Roll each stone away,
Keeping souls from God.

MY WORLD WITHIN.

I HAVE a little world I call my own,
No life of commonplace can claim its throne,
Far, far aloof from ponderous thought or care;
This calm retreat an angel e'en might share;
Perchance 't is found while floating o'er the sea,
Where dancing waves are tossing proud and free;
Or else 't is known when I, with book in hand,
Am pensive strolling o'er the pebbly sand.
No place, no occupation may conceal
Enjoyment which its treasured haunts reveal.
Such pleasant refuge is within my mind,
And there alone this little world I find.
Its walks serene, no poverty may reach,
No sheriff's summons cause the slightest breach;
The breath of scandal or the sneer of fools,
The plots of knav'ry with its shuffling tools,—

A rival's envy or the rich man's gold .
Their power to injure here no longer hold.
Far sooner may you scale the azure sky
Than touch this home from which all shadows fly.

CLOUDS.

HOW gently they float on the still twilight air,
In forms most mysterious, varied and rare ;
Now draped in vermilion or dappled in gold,
They seem all emblazoned with riches untold.
At midday how fleecily sail they above,
Like good angels watching in silence and love.
How densely they hover enshrouding the steep,
As tempests arise in their furious sweep ;
And when the deep thunderings cease to dismay,
How quickly they break 'neath the gladdening ray.
This world is a radiant world to our sight ;
Still, many a jetty cloud shuts out its light,
But glories will deck e'en the shadows most drear,
And make God's inscrutable providence clear;
And when towards life's evening the sun sinks to rest,
A bow will illumine the beautiful west.

LIVE IT DOWN.

HAS a foolish word been spoken,
  Or an evil deed been done;
Has the heart been almost broken,
  For the friends that now disown?
Let not coldness or the frown,
Shake thy manhood — live it down.

Is the stern traducer sneering,
  Thrusting innuendo vile,
With the world's opinion veering,
  Basking in its fickle smile?
What are gossips with their frown?
Buzzing insects — live it down.

Verdict fairer will be given,
  In the sober afterthought;
Charity, sweet child of Heaven,
  Judgment harsh will set at naught;
Then will grieved Mercy's frown
Smite the slanderer — live it down.

But if man refuse to soften,
  For that weakness he may feel,
There is One forgives us often,
  As to Him we choose to kneel;
Droop not then whoe'er may frown;
With such friendship — live it down.

STANLEY'S MARCH.

THE muse that lifts immortal strain to pure emprise
    and manly
Across the wave a tribute sends to note thy genius,
    Stanley !
As history will grave thy name with those that never
    perish,
So poesy reserves her right thy signal deeds to cherish.

The press fulfilled its mission high when choosing thee to
    banish
The shades enshrouding Afric's waste which at thy spell
    must vanish.
To ope the way for Christian light, revealing civic power,
To plant upon the serpent's head the heel, is now thy
    dower.

The mantle of a Livingstone, that master, is upon thee,
Reconsecrated for thy work, his spirit grand hath won
    thee.
Increasing motive presses close to make thy purpose
    stronger,
Till thou to meet thy life's intent canst seek the goal no
    longer.

Bold Stanley, on — complete the task defined by One
above thee,
Of science thou hast fondest wish, the prayers of those
that love thee.
Whatever be the coronal from earth's award receiving,
Thy sense of aid from God's right arm a deathless crown
is weaving.

LATER POEMS.

LATER POEMS.

★

OTONDA.

NOT long ago, by some now living seen, there
  grew a child,
Adorning like a flower or bird or laughing rill,
  a wild.
His hair as raven plumage black, and arrowy straight, fell
  o'er
An ample brow, whose outline grand the look of genius
  wore;
And honesty informed an eye that braved the face of day,
Though dreamy as the mist at times and soft as moonlight
  ray.
More agile scarce when climbing steep the lithe and bounding roe

165

Than he, nor yet more graceful as he learned to bend the
    bow.
In treaty for a plot of land, its boundary to describe,
A white man entertainment shared from members of his
    tribe.
Attracted by the presence of this charming Indian boy,
He wished to make him as his own, in ways of peace
    employ;
Would place him 'neath the influence of tutelage in town,
Where culture and example good might lift him to renown,
That like some tree from roughness hewn for purposes of art,
He might, when trimmed and polished, serve to fill a
    nobler part
Than that a forest training offered, incomplete the best,
That aimed at skill in hunting or for gory scalps in quest.
Through suavity and argument, made cogent by its style,
The white man tried from darkness this young pagan to
    beguile;
He sketched a glowing picture of the city where he dwelt,
He spoke of toys, confections, as adroit his way he felt,
Exciting fancies dormant in an undeveloped soul,
As wood ignited soon affects the hard and stolid coal;
And as the coal when once alive sends forth intenser heat,
Ambition, first unmoved, his heart with inspiration beat.

The child thus led to follow him, consent his parents gave,
In hopes to see their favorite among the whites a brave —
Presuming that as time rolled on to honor he would rise,
Which prejudice would flee before like tears that friendship
    dries,

Reflecting that they both ere long must reach life's setting
  sun,
While he whose happiness they sought, its course had just
  begun.
They knew this stranger well, that always friendly to their
  race
Whate'er he promised to perform no treachery would efface,
That kindness was a lodestar of his head and of his heart,
Which rendered them more willing with their child beloved
  to part.
Hence fervid benedictions by the aged pair were given,
Protectorship invoking that proceeds alone from Heaven,
Displaying such affection as in man or beast is found,
The sacred tie of earth — whereby celestials too are bound.

        To a different sphere Otonda went
          From the one he left behind;
        'T was a world of nature parted with,
          For a world by man designed;
        An adieu he bade to storm-lashed cliffs,
          Where I Am speaks through the cloud
        E'en above where eagles build their nests
          Which defy the plundering crowd;
        From the awe-inspiring cataract's roar
          And the brooklet's tuneful play,
        And the hunting-ground his fathers roamed,
          A preserve of choicest prey.
        He must leave profuse enameling flowers,
          And the only friends he knew;
        Yea, a home — at least a home to him
          With a love at all times true.

And for what exchange such haunts endeared,
Intertwined with earliest thought?
Upon what could boyish interest live,
When apart from scenes inwrought?
Upon nature cramped to senseless whim,
To the school of fashion tamed,
Her unique proportions scarce discerned,
By the latest edict maimed,
Where reduced to cold repression's will,
Unallowed to speak one's self,
The emotions full of import large
Are like books upon a shelf.
For a range where none his steps controlled
Through the almost boundless halls,
He must live confined where drooping forms
Are empaled by city walls.
For endurance born of simplest fare,
Undisturbed by heat or cold,
He must yield to softness luxury breeds,
That like serpent coils enfold.
He must risk disease from slightest cause,
As from sparks the fires that rage,
Where more quick ensue, from lust and wine,
The infirmities of age;
Though in reach of pleasures most men crave,
There must often be unrest
For the natal sports in fatherland,
For the free and open West.

In time the boy was taught to bear
His strange conditions through the care

And kindness of his guardians new,
Their guidance gentle as the dew.
To him the white man's wife was drawn,
Whose love went forth like sun at dawn,
To brighten until noonday glow,
As constant as the river's flow.
To wedded ones who ne'er have known
A child to bless the hours lone,
If such be sent, though alien born,
A void to fill in household lorn,
'T is like some timely balm that heals,
From unexpected source secured;
Within unfathomed depths it steals,
Awakening yearnings long immured.
Her husband, who Otonda brought,
And she were not with children blessed;
With joyousness they both were fraught
In finding this congenial guest.

Years gone, the youth forgot the past;
'T was like a dream that could not last,
Like tales within the wigwam told,
Departed memories of old.
As portion of the native stock
At length becomes the engrafted bough,
As molecule is changed to rock,
He seemed his race to disavow.

Up springs the lark from rustling brake,
Alert ambitious flight to take;

Thus mind in him essayed to rise,
And revel in expanding skies.
He soon had scope — for, sent to school,
The Indian by line and rule
Began a course — some post to fill
In future years through book-taught skill.
The foremost 'mid the ranks he moved
In education's steady march.
To others dark — to him 't was light,
Perceiving through acumen born,
Transmitted by ancestral life,
Where dissipation ne'er disturbed
The healthful tide of nature's law.
He mastered Greek and Latin roots,
At figures showed rare cleverness,
Wrote lucidly with flowing pen,
Declaimed with dignity and ease ;
He also, in athletic sports,
Showed muscle of resistless force;
In agonistic strife he reached
A gladiatorial mastery,
Each triumph toned by humbleness.

Successful thus, 't were passing strange
Had Envy prompt, delinquent proved.
On such occasion wide awake,
Like Satan she appeared at last,
With forked tongue ablaze with wrath.
The tawny skin and savage birth
Were stimulant to vent her spleen.

Professing him beneath contempt,
Out-distanced schoolmates oft reviled.
They taunted him with stinging words,
Which more than blows will sometimes wound;
Like Joseph's brethren in league,
Would e'en have killed had fear allowed.
Assured by patience, one more rash
The hated rival rudely struck.
At this the fury of his race
Shot forth with leonine effect;
With nerve sustained by anger pent,
His every blow with vigor told.
The leaders felled, a panic spread,
Which scattered all as flee the alarmed
When bursts the dreaded thunderbolt.

Ere long the dastard spirit, cowed,
Was changed to fawning compliment;
And he, so envied and abused,
A Hector or Achilles seemed.
The admiration secret felt
Was lavished on their conqueror;
And as the harrow breaks the sod
And smooths the ground for planting seed,
With bristling onslaught he subdued
The roughness of his future path.
And as the harrow fits the soil
Most hard for seed to germinate,
Good seed he caused to root, and grow
The fruits of wisdom, 'mongst his foes —

Beyond all cavil difference taught
'Twixt blustering and bravery.

The youth, advanced from school, to college went,
On higher education eager bent;
Its elements inwrought, he waxed athirst
In knowledge more recondite to be versed;
From Virgil, Xenophon, and Cicero,
To Plato, Livy, Homer would he go.

'T were needless in collegiate course to say
He foremost stood, as in the earlier day.
If character on principle be placed,
Its well-known record never is effaced,
Whate'er detraction loudly may proclaim
In futile effort to obscure a name;
But most when principle is guided by
That light which shines beyond the visual eye.

When time had elapsed to receive his degree,
On the stage he was chosen to speak;
An honor he honored whom all pressed to see,
As though he were wizard or freak.

Most glaring injustice imposed on his race,
The subject of rostrum or pen,
In romance was written, discussed in each place,
Resounding from city and glen.

Appropriate subject he culled for his theme
Was treatment the Indian incurred,
Where compact accepted, when candid 't would seem,
Agreement was only in word.   .

" The white man," he said,
" Has depleted our tribes;
From fastness to fastness they 're banished.
Immense tracts are ceded for trivial return,
Our lawful inheritance vanished.

" Our women and children a holocaust made
To suit the fierce Moloch of battle,
Affrighting the timid, the feeble, the halt,
We are robbed of our crops and our cattle.

" The poison of alcohol sold in our midst
Has opened worse sluices of sorrow.
This curse of the pale-face, its illness and crime,
From those who destroy us we borrow.

" Do war-whoop and tomahawk frighten your homes,
Dread ambuscade soldiers surprising?
As tiger beset in the jungle at bay,
Defense must be shrewd in devising."

When finished, an ocean-calm spread o'er the crowd,
Whose silence awhile was unbroken;
Applause then, like ocean's roar waked by the storm,
Of feeling profound was the token.

Of those who comprised the assembly that day
Was one who belonged to his people;
With war-paint and snake-rattle, plumage and beads,
O'er most there he towered like a steeple.

For leagues had he traveled Otonda to find,
Directed to where he was speaking;
Whom, when he perceived, with a wish to upbraid
His spirit tumultuous was reeking.

When all were retiring, each duty performed,
Came forward the wrath-smitten stranger;
He greeted the hero, who sprang from his tribe,
With a look and a voice full of danger.

Remembering the tongue which he spoke as a child,
The import of words now ejected
The civilized son of the forest discerned,
His slumbering nature affected.

" You 've left us, though bloodhounds have scented
    our trail,
Deserted a father and mother;
With war-notes resounding, the enemy near,
You 're far from your post," spake the other.

" The time must arrive when the white man will change
Toward one a mere plaything of humor;
Detested our race, he will cast you aside,
At spur of a whim or a rumor.

" Break loose from encumbrances none should endure,
From chains in which falsehood has bound you;
Be free once again where great forests invite
Unmortgaged dominion around you."

Impressed by such rally to duty, and dreams
Of hopes he had weakly forsaken,
And ennuied by customs till lately unknown,
Advice of the stranger was taken.

Within his breast a conflict raged
Like good and evil in the soul,
His Christian nurture first prevailed,
Then wilder impulse had control.

Another Indian not unlike,
Who high a West Point graduate stood,
When once a soldier in the field
Evinced the native thirst for blood.

Amid the strife his war-whoop rang,
Which startled comrades standing by;
And scalps from enemies secured
With gloating joy he lifted high.

. . . . .

It grieved him sore to bid farewell
To foster-parents loved as kind,
Who pointed to the endless life,
Supplanting base idolatry.
He sadly turned from those who gave
The mental appetite its food,

Whose hunger met has decked the world
With stars of magnitude the first,
And breaks the chain of slavery,
Which taint of birth, ignoble, mocks,
Unclogging evolution's wheel,
As tireless as the chariot steeds
Wherewith Aurora brings the morn.

At fiat spoken tears were shed
By those who long had called him son;
They told him should his purpose change
Complexion from its dismal hue,
And retrogressive step repair
To haunts that now had lost their hold,
He ne'er should find the threshold frown
As he approached; but open arms
Would greet the absent one, as though
Unslighted, tender guardianship.

From civilized restraint set free,
Otonda hied to whence he came,
The place he deemed as once 't was known,
Illumined by his fancy's flame.
Thus oft we gild our childhood's haunts
When years have shut them from our view,
Forgetting that the earlier taste
Was vastly different from the new.
The Mississippi broad they passed,
The buttonwood upon its bank,
In midst of thickest forest plunged,

And waded through the morass dank;
O'er prairies trod, the Rockies neared,
Where grouse and buffalo defied
The hunter's bullet from the East,
Where sportsman's skill was seldom tried.
At last the curling smoke betrayed
The hut of aborigines,
Where venison dried and calumet
And arrowhead one often sees.

Otonda to his people came,
But far their wigwams were removed—
Supplanted by progression's foot,
He missed the places first he knew.
He saw in early crudeness man,
Primeval, scarcely touched by art,
Not half-way in development,
But seeming almost at the start.

Before him hung the spoils of war,
A gruesome show on every side,
The silken locks once careful dressed
By maiden or by luckless bride.

Uncouth the habits that prevailed
In food, in person, in attire;
Long used to ways of cleanliness,
He shrank with loathing at the mire.

Not told by comrade reticent, he learned
His father and his mother both were gone
Before the fullness of last August's moon,
Earth's destiny attained—their work was done.

A sadness overcame his deep disgust—
For they to him were parents sealed by blood;
Harsh death his purpose mocked—to smooth the way
Ere life's canoe had reached its final flood.

What fellowship hath Christ with Belial,
Or darkness, error's friend, with virtue's light?
Can two together walk except agreed?
Have birds of plumage different, common flight?
His every feeling militant forbade
Communion with such grossness unrestrained;
Yet while a dissonance so marked he felt,
Otonda pitying friendship still retained.

The student fresh from his scholastic walks,
By intercourse select, refined,
Not bred to sleep at last 'mong Indian mounds—
For Academic groves far distant pined.

The bond of parentage by death dissolved,
Removing every hindrance to his bent,
A voice within intruded on repose
Until returning was his sole intent.

Not many days remaining with his tribe,
Of whom but few in childhood he had known,
He rode upon the wing of buoyant hope
To reap the harvest that his toil had sown.

And going where adoption's lessened power
Was shaken by a red man's fervid plea,
Adoption re-arose in pristine strength,
As will relented in a like degree.

The throbbing breast of love that never fails
Increased its largess as attachment grew!
And him, by absence only nearer brought,
Its yielding tenderness the closer drew.

Delighted guardians welcomed his return,
And thus fulfilled their promise ere he left.
Each token in his room remained the same,
As though of him they ne'er had been bereft.

Desiring some vocation to pursue,
Nor wishing on indulgence to depend,
Among the liberal three, the law his choice,
Agreeable to wish and mental trend.

Deciding thus, instruction he received
'Neath guidance of a well-known advocate,
Who as the sun makes earth to fructify
Did he this budding mind accelerate.

He mastered Chitty, Coke and Story, Kent;
Dry documents could draw, and learned to moot:
In Cupid's court he also proved adept,
O'erruled demurrer and pressed on his suit.

The daughter of the lawyer waked the flame
That kindled feeling unaroused before,
Whose golden curls and tender eyes of blue
A contrast to his dusky visage bore.

Affection sought and found a hidden spell
Its potency unveiled by look or speech;
It found a heaven-breathing sentiment
That alien effort could not mar nor reach.

He saw companionship for leisure hours
When care like withered leaves from thoughts we
    shake,
He saw companionship for troubled hours
With everything we hold most dear at stake.

In mood poetic he composed these lines,
Descriptive of impression she had made:
Accompanied by notes of the guitar,
They oft had charmed when falls the evening shade.

SONG.

" I love thee for thy beaming eye,
    Thy thrilling voice, thy smile;
But better far I love thee, dear,
    For words that ne'er beguile.

" I love thee for the tresses which
  Thy brow serene enwreath,
But ah, my soul receives delight
  From thoughts so pure beneath.

" I love thee for thy artlessness,
  The graces of thy form;
But much more for a spirit true
  In sunshine and in storm.

" I love thee for the quiet joy
  Thy presence doth impart,
But most I prize thee for that gem —
  A woman's faithful heart."

He that weds for heart and mind
True happiness is sure to find;
He that only beauty woos
Will learn that love is blind.
When entrapped by coin alone,
The bread he asks becomes a stone;
If pomp and state the nuptial aim,
He chance may win an empty name.
A kingdom but a bauble seems
With such a cheating fate;
Far better unknown peasant's lot
Who dwells in neat and humble cot
Contented with his mate.

As sculpture lends to marble cold
A grace that wins approving eye,
So two with love, though lot obscure,
May beauty know that cannot die.

Alas! the current of a tide
Is changed in unexpected ways;
When smoothest flows the joyous stream,
Some wildering storm its promise stays.

Otonda, more than blessed thus far,
His pathway purpled o'er by hope,
Must learn how vain is fortune's dream,
How truthless earthly horoscope.

In time he sought the father's ear,
Petitioned for the daughter's hand,
Well knowing suit but null and void
Unless approved by his command.

A frown spread o'er the parent's brow
When the suggestion first was made —
Though fault in him he could not tell,
He thought such union would degrade.

A blank refusal was received;
It gave an unexpected shock,—
An arrow driven in his breast
Could scarce more rude his feelings mock.

The lawyer to Otonda said :
" Take cordial wishes for success —
At home or at your work engaged,
May Providence your pathway bless.

" Of different race from mine you came,
By courtesy with us you dwell;
If wedded to my daughter — now
'T were ill — the future who could tell ? "

'T was not alone refusal given
In words so terrible to hear,
'T was slur upon his origin
That brake most harshly on his ear:

That effort would in vain attempt
Race prejudice to keep at bay,
The castle he had fondly built
Must 'neath its fury melt away.

He felt, though innocent, a brand
Like Cain's was stamped upon his brow,
That shunned and hated, though admired,
To man's unfairness he must bow.

.   .   .   .   .

Half crazed, he westward turned his face,
And soon was lost amid the wood;
For days and nights he scarcely paused
Till near a river vast he stood.

Then gazing on those waters dark,
Beneath whose depths De Soto sleeps,
One plunge he made — a great soul gone,
Until his just award he reaps.

So hearts may break and men may die
Through blows of brutal ignorance;
But love will live and cannot lie,
Though hard and sad the sweet romance.

'T were idle to portray her grief
Who longest must its draught imbibe;
'T is said that, crushed, she found relief
In self-devotion to his tribe.

But let us turn from minor key
And harp upon more pleasant theme;
Awake from sloth, Philanthropy,
Cheer up, advance thy favored scheme.

For now Minerva walks abroad,
And bloody Mars lays down his sword;
The race a Pocahontas bred
By Christian hands is gently led.

Atlantic and Pacific tides
Lave shores where not, as once, abides
Race prejudice; and all may see
By mind is measured dignity.

Behold! a camp-fire cheerful burns
To cheat the darkness and the chilliness of night,
As, in a world of gloom from sin
And superstition shrouding truth, beams gospel light.

The wigwam stately palace shames,
Which small may satisfy a humble mortal's wish;
And game, the mark of huntsman's skill,
Is wide bestrewn — no richer on Lucullus' dish.

Grotesque are seen in gay attire
The red man and his squaw with slumbering papoose —
The halo of religion o'er,
Uplifting from the slough of moral notions loose.

And as the queen of night that shines
To gladden and to beautify 'mid moving spheres —
Like Dorcas or like Lydia,
Our heroine, exhorting them, a saint appears.

Be calm thy rest, Otonda, then,
As depth of Mississippi on a genial day;
Thy mission is fulfilled in her
Whose soul is thine, although thy image be away.

THE LION'S FEAST.

THE lion, famed as king of beasts,— the noblest of them
    all,—
Will yet, as oft with royalty, play tricks both great and small;
Nay, sometimes like grimalkin, if intent upon his prey,
So slyly steal along that none suspect him in the way.

He sent an invitation once to animals around,
Requesting they would feast within his palace under ground.
Most flattering! They could share such spoils as princely
        thieves can boast,
While their rapacious enemy would smile, a gentle host!

This courtesy by most of them was joyfully received:
If dubious the motive, his professions they believed.
The fox, and other knowing ones, refused a lion's dish:
They felt a chill suspicion of design beneath his wish.

Complacent was the forest's lord at progress of his scheme,
Most carefully dissembled lest murder it might seem;
So low was now his larder that few fragments were at hand,
While thus supply might be obtained — the choicest in the
    land.

Down went the guileless quadrupeds to dine in regal state,
Not thinking that their carcasses his appetite would sate:
The donkey, rabbit, mole, the deer, the sloth, the goat,
   the sheep —
A jocund party, in his lair high festival to keep!

Most affable yet dignified, he greeted every guest,
As one by one they filed along to answer his behest.
He looked a kind approval, but his teeth were shown
   quite plain —
They trembled, though he did not roar, but merely shook
   his mane.

Among them soon a panic spread, perceiving no repast,
But, freely scattered, well-picked bones, that made them
   stand aghast.
Invectives at their foe they hurled, deluded by a snare —
His lamb-like mood accounted for, his infamy laid bare.

The lion 'mid their obloquy would justify his end,
A plot most diabolical audaciously defend;
With sophistry expounded why he bade them to his
   cave,
Where all, at mercy of his will, were far from chance to
   save.

" E'en animal most virtuous," said he, " would act the same
As I have done, if hungry and enticed by tempting game.
To stratagem resorting also you your prey secure —
No crookedness a hindrance, if to catch it feeling sure.

"Besides, I am the King of beasts, who, when the ground
    I paw
And lift my voice, can hold the trembling forest leaves
    in awe:
'T is also my prerogative, unquestioned autocrat,
To treat my subjects as I please — from elephant to rat.

"As man alone inferior creation may control,
Thus lord of life and death to all dependents I am sole.
Moreover, executioner who law's demand exalts,
Offenders I destroy whene'er debased by hopeless faults."

At which bold speech his victims, rendered desperate by
    fear,
Essayed most ardent pleas to urge — a grim tribunal near:
Although perchance aware that they were hoping against
    hope,
Yet protestation offered they, within permissive scope.

The donkey spoke: "Please name some cause why I
    should be destroyed —
A burden-bearer, scolded, whipped, pray whom have
    I annoyed?"
"O stupid creature," said the lion, "neither coaxed nor
    driven;
With pointed steel, despite your bray, your vitals should
    be riven."

With tearful eye his purity the graceful deer averred,
Whose eloquence, with longing tooth, the Judge reluctant heard.
"Weak fop," he said, "in love with self, reflected in the
brook,
Such emptiness decides your fate, though guileless you
may look."

No word they uttered could avail to check his bloody task;
And all of them, disheartened, ceased his clemency to ask.
Not long before the King began his subjects each to slay,
The average amounting to one animal per day.

Much royal condescension is mistrusted by the wise;
While simpletons are soon entrapped, as by the spider flies.
The lion, as of right, will always keep a lion's share —
To suit his savage purposes, his hapless victims tear.

So demagogue political will feign a savory feast,
Inviting his constituents, with cunning like this beast;
Or wily mining expert, with his billion corporate stock,
Inflate a golden bubble till it burst with bankrupt-shock;

Or delegate in purple oft — though workmen be in rags —
Call out his Knights of Labor, to supply his money-bags.
Well fed upon a stipend, he can laugh within his sleeve,
As Folly strikes for Slavery, while wives and children
grieve.

A WORD.

NO word is lost when once 't is spoken,
  But echoes on the air;
Although to fragments sometimes broken,
  Its sound can naught impair.
It travels to remotest regions,
  A spirit of unrest,
Companion of the vocal legions
  Like birds without a nest.

A word may make the culprit tremble,
  And bid his color flee,
When judge and jury grave assemble
  And " guilty " the decree.
A word may make the saddened cheerful
  When held in durance vile :
If pardon be proclamed, the tearful
  No longer weep, but smile.

When overcome by anxious feeling,
  Long tossed upon the deep,
If " land " from one aloft be pealing
  Our fears are put to sleep.
When war protracted scourges nations,
  Nor hopes of truce arise,
A voice resounds to generations
  When " peace " salutes the skies.

The yes or no by lovers uttered
  A destiny foretells;
Domestic storms to come are muttered,
  Or angel music swells.
A word will states or nations sunder,
  Raise high or dash to earth,
Like lightning scathe, alarm as thunder,
  Abundance cause or dearth.

'T is like the dynamite that shatters
  The deep primeval rock,
And aged fossils ruthless scatters
  In one appalling shock;
Or like the dynamite that blesses
  And not alone destroys —
A force by which the world progresses,
  Imparting nameless joys.

Perchance a word we now remember
  Of one long passed away;
It comes back in our life's December,
  A blossom of its May.
Not volumes with such gentle power
  The depths of being wake —
'T will linger to the latest hour
  For that loved sleeper's sake.

SALVATION — other words excelling —
  Throughout the Gospel shines;
Its promise mercy's lips are telling
  To lift each heart that pines.

Beyond the firmament, pervasive,
  Outvoicing Ocean's roar,
Beams this celestial term persuasive
  That fills the evermore.

THE DAUGHTERS OF THE REVOLUTION.

OF ancestry ye came not
    The mock of tyrant will,
Whose deeds of blood we name not —
Mere puppets bought to kill.

Your sires strove not for plunder,
The glamour of applause —
They rushed 'mid warfare's thunder
For freedom's noblest cause.

They fought to slay all fighting,
To build the throne of peace,
A present wrong were righting
That future wrong might cease.

And mothers may ye boast of
Who fired the patriot heart;
Such dames there was a host of,
Each equal to her part.

They graced the humble kitchen,
And parlor too as well,
As jagged rocks the lichen,
Or flowers grace the dell.

From wheel and distaff plying
The harpsichord they sought,
In plainest garment vying
As though of gold 't were wrought.

As lily in the valley
Delights the scene around,
From darkness did they rally —
A joy 'mid grief profound.

Ye honored as descendants,
Exalt the name ye bear;
Be liberty's defendants,
Adorn the badge ye wear.

'Mid national declension
Through luxury and pride,
With timely intervention
Roll back each trait'rous tide.

No overgrowth can harm us
If woman interpose;
From threatening evil charm us,
And Yorktown's chief disclose.

Unrivaled is your mission,
Which heedless ye profane;
'T is worthy all ambition —
Its source without a stain.

TO THE CAPITOL AT WASHINGTON.

THY classic dome in solemn worship greets the sky,
  No envying shadow dims the noonday sun,
    The candid light
    Shows marble white
'Neath which the destinies of millions lie
In Continental Congress erst begun.

Serene thou smilest 'mid each conflict rude of state
  Which like a whirlwind shocks the peaceful soul,
    Rebuking those
    Mere useless floes
Who block progression's tide by party hate,
Whom sordid, not their country's, aims control.

Fair Capitol, canst not through art to truth allure,
  Such harmony in thy proportions grand,
    With columns just
    Near patriot bust,
With Doric and Corinthian model pure,
Conceived where genius stayed barbaric hand.

If they who law devise to meet a people's need
  Forget their weal who lifted them to place,
      'Gainst vile unrest
      Wilt thou protest,
  Like virtue ever scattering wholesome seed
  Where clamorous self the spirit's shrine disgrace.

A group of sisters does the nation's flag entwine,
  As differing parts the human form compose;
      So ever hold
      As one enrolled
  The stars upon our heritage divine
  Which with consentient will at first uprose.

No Pantheon of multifarious creeds art thou,
  Where war religions brought from every land—
      Thy storied walls
      Assembly halls
  Respecting each conviction's honest vow—
  A monument to Freedom thou shalt stand.

GENERAL VON MOLTKE.

AT THE AGE OF NINETY.

SOME iron men there be
That stand as bulwarks in defense of
country or of right;
The deepest gloom brings forth their light,
A torch of victory.
These Nestors come we know not whence
Amid suspense.

Von Moltke silent, famed
For action, not for boastful word, stands thus among the few
Which Austria, France, and Denmark knew.
Both great and good is named
This chief of council and the sword
So wide adored.

Unflinching Bismarck towers,
And so the conqueror renowned — that youth may borrow
heart,
Learn virtues that 'mid peace depart.
To summon patriot powers
These living monuments are found
Of record sound.

We all incentive need
From signals of a well-spent past, those heroes that were wont
'Mid thickening shot to brave the front,
Not born to follow, but to lead,—
Whose stalwart lives, achievements vast,
Will time outlast.

LORD TENNYSON.

IN beauty and monition lifts the tall cathedral spire,
A waymark for each pilgrim who makes earth or
heaven his goal:
So upward wreathes and faithful points thy true poetic fire,
A lofty guide for earthly art, or thought that wakes the
soul.

THE SEVENTIETH BIRTHDAY OF WILLIAM TECUMSEH SHERMAN.

THE sands of life run golden,
Telling hours away;
With God are we beholden
To waste not by delay.

He oft prolongs the season,
    Work to do complete,
Till force or will or reason
    Makes end and purpose meet.

'T is well ripe age is given
    One whom honor claims;
His compeers speak from Heaven,
    His toil the sluggard shames.

To duty's voice he yielded,
    Startling Georgia's shore;
The cause of man he shielded
    Till arms could do no more.

And now is he fulfilling
    Gentle calls of peace;
A kindly power distilling
    That nevermore will cease.

As feared by foes opposing,
    Loved he is by friends;
Warm greetings now disclosing
    The spell his presence lends.

May countless years still cluster,
    Health and joy remain,
Before the final muster
    The unseen heights to gain.

NOVEMBER MUSINGS.

THE withered and the falling leaf
  O'er hill and plain is scattered:
It tells us, like the golden sheaf,
  How summer dreams are shattered.

The winds more chilly sweep along,
  Where flowers have departed,
And scarce we hear the wood-bird's song,
  While comrades south have started.

Proud beauty, throned in gorgeous prime,
  With freshness was surrounded;
Her pomp subdued suggests the time
  When wintry blasts are sounded.

Reflection, pondering that sleep
  To which we all are hasting,
Recalls the fruits we failed to reap,
  Probation's moments wasting.

But autumn leaves with brilliant hues
  Cheat Nature of her sadness;
Illusion charms the soul that views,
  Till sighs are lost in gladness.

And though we trace the lessening bloom
That warns us of life's ending,
Through faith some power will banish gloom,
A radiant beam descending.

MY FRIEND.

I HAVE a true Friend, far distant his home,
And yet at my bidding most willing to come.
    With him may be found
    A balm for each wound
Afflicting — as over life's desert we roam.

With nothing below the spirit to cheer,
To bring back the smile and to banish the tear,
    He reaches the soul
    Which sorrows control,
And makes above darkness the light to appear.

When summer friends go, like glare of the day,
Who only are wont with the prosp'rous to stay,
    He constant remains,
    And love still retains,
More closely adhering as these haste away.

How swift speed the hours like arrows that glide,
While many the cherished who fall by our side;
    Yet One may be seen
    With visage serene,
A lightship that floats 'mid the stormiest tide.

When evening draws on, and Nature seeks rest,
He sends forth his angels whom none can molest;
    Such sentry disarms
    All foes or alarms,
If Faith make its pillow a Saviour's breast.

And when at the last this earth we shall leave,
And bidding farewell, loved and loving must grieve,
    The soul he uplifts,
    And shows us bright rifts
In clouds against heaven our doubts interweave.

THE DREADED ISLAND.

AS toward yon distant isle the helmsmen steer,
  In every bosom is awakened fear;
    Forbidding rocks arise
    To anxious eyes;
  And shoals — like treacherous foes,
Concealed by noiseless billows, none would think
    were near — lie hid.
If harmlessly the wave repose,
  Or fatally the tempest sweep
And lash to fury far and wide
  The wayward and remorseless deep —
The lurid lightning danger writes upon the tide,
Where fathoms down doth many a bark
    Lie desolate, and none can know
Where absent loved ones sleep.

When night spreads shadows dark
   Soon furled is every sail,
      While hearts more timorous grow,
   An unknown fate bewail.

   Upon this island food is placed,
That when, perchance, is lost some hapless ship
   The saved may live till, fear effaced,
By timely aid they may resume their trip,
   And reach some safer shore,
   Where terrors they have felt may ne'er affrighten more.

   'Mid fairest seeming, fatal isles doth life disclose,
Our trend is toward them like the needle to the pole.
      Unrippling silent waves that glow
   Allay suspicion and the thought of dole.
   Succeedeth rashness, when the helm of wisdom ceases
      to control —
Unquestioning do mortals steer to where the subtle evils lie,
Though many wrecks to make them pause may they descry,
And tales of navigators thwarted bid them fly.

Still safety may they find who on these rocks are cast,
They yet may live, albeit destruction seem to bind the
      victim fast.
            A God is there,
            As everywhere,
            And when they strive,
            He keeps alive.

An antidote removes the bane;
A lifted prayer, and man is safe again.
He rescues, who a Peter kept from watery grave,
And taught his timid follower to tread the stormy
wave.

REVERIES ON VIRGINIA BEACH.

I WANDER o'er Virginia Beach,
Whose length is more than eye can reach,
Where laboring footsteps patience teach.
I watch the ocean's changeful hue,
Its tints of brown and green and blue,
While moving sails oft meet the view.

I see a wreck upon the sand,
Her hull yet sound, proportions grand,
Though rudely hurled by Neptune's hand.
How sad to think of, outward bound,
Some promised dreamland never found —
Of beauteous forms by seaweed wound!

Again, I see a broken net,
Like shattered wishes never met,
Though gleesome woven seines were set.
On pebbles smooth or glistening shell
My wandering glance doth often dwell;
They seem of greetings kind to tell.

I see a white bird cast ashore:
Its shattered wing is stained with gore;
It ne'er can skim the ether more.
So whiter seems a life when flown,
And Envy leaves its prey alone:
By crimson stain 't is purer known.

No more the sportive naiads lave;
The power of God is in yon wave —
'T is he alone the soul can save.
The noblest thought, in noblest speech,
Hath not such gift the heart to teach
As voices from Virginia Beach.

THE FLOWERS IN BOSTON PUBLIC GARDEN.

O BOSTON, city of the past and of the living present,
   With fancies decked in hues as rich as those of
      golden pheasant,
Whose transcendentalism, like thy streets, seems very mazy,
Or like the fogs upon near coasts — conspicuously hazy.

Of all the sights to waken thought amid thy many glories,
Thy monuments and statues, linked with patriotic stories,
Naught captivates and charms us more than flowers fair
    adorning
Thy Public Garden, radiant with freshness of the morning.

The tuberose and the hyacinth and pink delight the senses,
Where Nature, trained by human skill, her fragrance rare
    dispenses.
Each army corps its badge may claim, the hand of taste
    displaying;
Deserting its allotted sphere, we find no leaflet straying.

Like regiments in phalanx close, appropriate their draping,
'T would seem some orderly with care attended to their
    shaping.
A tear arises in his eye, who fought to save the nation,
When these sweet emblems bid him pause amid his
    recreation.

Instructors that dispel from life the shades which often
    lower,
Upon this day of import deep thus teach by thine own
    power:
Our country in her proud advance, her splendor and her
    sinning,
Needs hearts as true and hands as brave as those at her
    beginning.

GRAND ARMY DAY, Aug. 12, 1890.

A DOG'S DEATH.

ONE morning a dog, with his fate not content,
    Disgusted with three years of life,
To where rushed the train at a rail-crossing went,
    Determined to end fortune's strife.

Unconscious of fear, on the iron he lay,
    Though danger was at its full height,
With scarcely a moment the past to survey,
    His limbs and his sorrows took flight.

Soon after his master perceived the remains
    Of Fido, to household endeared,
Which, having entombed with solicitous pains,
    A monument worthy he reared.

Alas, like a dog's is the lot of our race,
    The world whipping much at its will;
And if, like the dog, no design could we trace,
    The suicide's grave more would fill.

In buffetings wisdom sees purposes high,
    The sweet fruits of patience in view;
'Neath blows, while the foolish then curse God and die,
    Their lives will the thoughtful renew.

THE LORD'S PRAYER.

FATHER, thou who art in heaven,
    Hallowed be thy name,
May thy kingdom's peaceful leaven
    War disarmed proclaim;
May thy will, which man resisting,
    From himself ne'er won,
Through the earth be still persisting
    As on high 't is done.
Thou, who countless souls art feeding,
    Give us daily bread;
Let each one who food is needing
    Share thy bounty spread.
Wrong forgive by us committed
    In thy holy sight,
As thy servants have remitted
    Trespass 'gainst their right.
'Mid temptation lead us never,
    Evil's work undo,
For thy kingdom standeth ever,
    Power, glory, too.   Amen.

RAIN.

DROP, drop, rain, rain,
    A priceless boon thou art;
A greeting sends the arid plain,
    The shallow brook, the mart.

Attending breezes cool the brow,
　The blinding dust allayed —
Thy crystal purity on bough
　And mead and tender blade.

A gift I have, a favorite plant
　Which by yon lattice springs;
Its faded beauties seem to pant,
　To droop like wearied wings.

O prithee, rain, my spirit cheer,
　And ere too late revive
Its growth, and bring the giver near
　To bid affection thrive.

How rhythmic at the midnight hour
　Thy pattering on the roof,
While slumber owns thy soothing power,
　To druggist's art reproof!

To every mortal thou art kind —
　The just and unjust too;
For mercy we can never bind,
　Whatever ill we do.

Impatience oft would drive thee hence,
　Provided long thy stay;
Reflection yields, regardful whence
　The bread consumed each day.

In season due thy moistened tread
  Along the town or wood;
The harvest ripe, the harvest dead,
  Thy path bestrewn with good.

As they who weep return with sheaves
  Of joyousness again,
O tearful sky, thy blessings leave
  To hinder Famine's pain.

Our prayers be like ascending mist
  That calls down fruitful showers;
May Grace their fervency assist,
  And change life's dearth to flowers.

MY CANARY.

'TWAS given to me
  By one o'er the sea,—
So precious, though wee,—
      My Canary!
O'erlooked from his size —
Yet, blinking his eyes,
He seemed very wise —
      My Canary!

And this pretty thing
With bright yellow wing
Most sweetly would sing —
      My Canary!

Ah, sad was the night!
A mouse with a bite
Removed my delight—
       My Canary!

I saw him ere dead:
He chirruped, raised his head,
And then his life fled—
       My Canary!

Lone days will prolong
That last note of song,
That eve's cruel wrong—
       My Canary!

TO A FRIEND AFTER A LONG ABSENCE.

I SAW thee not as in the youthful past
  With maiden beauty of unwonted kind,—
Such charms could not forever last,
Since years roll on and leave their marks behind.
I saw thee when the brown to white had turned,
And traces of life's discipline were shown—
When, though the altar flame of love still burned,
Yet by affection more subdued 't was known.
Still beauty rested on thy brow serene,
As sunlight peering through a softening cloud,
Suggestive more than when in girlhood seen,
Like music faintly heard — not near and loud.

Dear friends of youth, how magical their power!
They waken visions which can never die :
We do not view them as a transient flower,
But like the leaves which in some volume lie.
May time add blessings to thy wedded store,
Their sources deepening in a love-lit home,
Till thou in peace shalt reach the open door
Where undimmed friendship crowns the life to come!

THE HORSE.

L ITHE doth he bound,
Spurning the ground;
Graceful each curve
Quivering with nerve :
A creature of beauty from fetlock to mane,
The full-blooded steed as he courses the plain.

Taskmasters ply
Burdens that try
Patience and brawn,
Plodding from dawn :
Of all useful creatures he serves man the best,
Most worthily claiming his food and his rest.

Proud but yet meek,
Love does he seek;
Scarcely when heard,
Swayed by a word :
His head tossed with anger, impetuous, wild —
Caressed, he will stoop to the hand of a child.

Intellect's light
Smiles through brute night;
Fineness of tact
Lurks in an act:
" He smelleth the battle afar off," and breathes
A craving for laurels that victory wreathes.

Praise of the horse
Ages endorse,
Beauteous with might,
Gentle and bright:
Bucephalus high amid chargers in fame
A prestige hath given an undying name.

THE ENGLISHMAN AND THE SCOT.

AN Englishman on Scotia's soil,
Where Nature's barrenness defies mere toil,
Surprised, was at a loss to trace
By what devices she maintained her race.
While musing o'er a sterile heath,
With frowning skies above and rocks beneath,
A native did he thus address:
" With special favor Heaven seems to bless
You Northmen, save in choice of food.
Pray tell me how you live?" In jesting mood
He asked; then waited for reply.
" On oatmeal," said the Scot, " do we rely."

At this response the Southron smiled.
Grown portly with rich fare, he deemed it wild.
" On oatmeal we our horses feed,"
He said, while roast-beef visions moved his greed.
The Scot rejoined, in tone of glee :
" What horses do you raise ! — what men do we ! "

TO A DISTINGUISHED PHYSICIAN ON HIS
SEVENTY-SECOND BIRTHDAY.

BUT few are the sheaves which the life reaper brings
   When the chances to glean are departing,
Compared with those promised when Hope spread
      her wings
'Mid illusions of youth at the starting.

Not thus 't is with thee in thy ripeness of years
   Long renowned in the province of healing;
The good thou hast done in Time's record appears,
   Ample measure its pages revealing.

The poor with the rich whom thy art has made glad
   Now the tokens of love are presenting :
They trust that thy smile and thy skill to the sad
   Yet may bless, pain's intrusion preventing.

This tribute accept of a friend's deep regard
  Thou hast cheered amid sickness and sorrow;
God grant thee above an eternal reward,
  And below, oft a happy to-morrow.

DOES THE POET LIVE?

A CRITIC mourns the Muse as dead and buried —
  That this prosaic age, engrossed in traffic,
Has quenched the flame that burned so bright on Scio —
Rekindled and more lambent yet on Avon :
Apollo's lyre is dumb before the harshness
Of car and steamer whistle, loom and shuttle.
He says, "Though rhymers may abound — not poets,"—
Inferior as the second-temple offerings,
Which seem like flowers scattered on a highway
Downtrodden and unworthy to be gathered,—
That bards who wake the strain sublime have vanished,—
That 'mid the Babylon of grasping commerce,
Held captive by its chain, their harps are idle.

Plain common sense repels the imputation;
It finds the Muse prolific now as ever;
A higher standard are its numbers reaching —
That greater lights are dimmed by many great ones,
While few competing better chance gave genius.

Does music longer flourish, or does painting ?
Let crowds decide who press to hear a Patti,

And wealth that on a Meissonier was lavished —
For art is single though its kin are many.
As soon may droop forever rose or lily,
Their bloom and fragrance fail to please the senses;
Niagara as soon may roar unheeded,
His mountains cease to stir the pride of Switzer;
As soon the stars may fail to make us wonder,
Or night gloom, coming fancies weird to conjure;
As soon may Cupid break his bow and slumber,
May smiles and tears no longer cheer or sadden,
As ever Poetry forget her mission,
Nor longer lift from troubled hearts their burden.

THE OCTOGENARIAN'S LAMENT.

WHEN I am gone who will care?
   My loss the world will soon repair.
Perchance my dog will whine and look more sad —
   I 'm sure my absence will not drive him mad;
The cat when on my lounge may purr the more,
   Less oft awhile my bird his strains may pour;
But onward will the car of time proceed
   As though the world did not my presence need.

Beside these pets some may care:
   The one for whom I cleared the air
From scandal's pestilence of envy born
   Where reputation was of honor shorn;

The poor I 've helped, and those whom I 've consoled
When 'mid a heart-felt grief but few condoled;
And they may mourn who, blind to every fault,
The humblest virtue that I have exalt.

When I am gone some will care—
It may be but the instance rare
Of those whose love is more than in the name,
Who when I greet them ever are the same,
Unlike the changelings of the hour that smile
Yet frown as quick when interest's voice beguile:
Such ties will cheer the gloom the grave must bring
Like nightingales that make the darkness ring.

LET DOWN THE BARS.

L ET down the bars — for twilight's fleeting hour
   Is deepening shadows in the somber vale;
The robin in the copse has ceased his singing;
   The owl will soon go forth and nightingale.

Let down the bars — the golden-rod and cowslip,
   The buttercup, the clover, and the fern
Must quick retire from flaunting day's exposure
   To sip the cooling dews at eve's return.

Let down the bars — the maid in restless humor
   With foaming white the empty pail would fill;
All clean the pans within the dairy glistening;
   The churn, tho' ready for its work, is still.

Let down the bars — the cattle sauntering homeward,
　But faintly will their tinkling bells be heard;
Beneath its wing the sheltering night enfolding
　Repose will give to man and beast and bird.

Let down the bars, we say, 'mid earthly pastures,
　When sighing for the herbage ever green,
Whene'er for " waters still " the soul is panting —
　The living waters of the land unseen.

"THE FAR-AWAY LOOK."

WHY, maiden, that mysterious look so rapt and far
　away,
As though intent on distant scenes that hold thee by
　their sway ?
Why deaf to duty's noble call, which needs thy every care,
　While gazing on the listless cloud or on the empty air?

Is meditation lured to one with thoughts akin to thine,
　To whom affection firmly clings, as to the oak the vine ?
Art thou absorbed in him who seems like hilltop o'er the
　vale,
　Or sparkling ore that miners, with an untold pleasure,
　hail ?

Does poet-flame illume within and send its beam afar,
　Thine eye bewildered shining like some lone and errant
　star ?

Enravished by Apollo's lyre, that charms Parnassus' height,
  Doth soar on wings of fame to perch where genius aims
    its flight ?

Art weaving hopes like frost-work, or like shadows on the
    wall,
  With youth-inspired vision that forebodings ne'er appal ?
Does life suggest a fairy-land, remote from fear or pain,
  The bright side of its pattern seen, obscured its rough
    and plain ?

Has sorrow dashed the promise that shed calmness on thy
    brow,
  The burden of to-morrow or the falsehood of a vow ?
Dost ponder o'er the gloom which oft surmounts the
    gladdest day,
  And hence the strange mysterious look — that look so
    far away ?

Perhaps the soul immortal, which adds beauty to thine eye,
  Would from its earthly prison-house some Ararat
    descry —
Would lend its fair possessor the true rest for hopes and
    dreams,
  Where every picture Faith unfolds is lovelier than it
    seems.

THE WACCAMAW.

MY heart returns to long ago,
  Recalls a river's gentle flow,
That oft-reflected pleasure's glow:
This river loved, I daily saw
And floated o'er — the Waccamaw.

Where skyward points the Southern pine,
With other tides its waves combine
As souls congenial oft entwine:
They tell of love's mysterious law,
These streamlets with the Waccamaw.

Upon its margin roses grew,
Like those Cashmere unfolds to view
As smiling 'mid the morning dew:
Their crimson leaves with scarce a flaw
Were fragrant near the Waccamaw.

The old plantation cheers the past,
Whose memories will time outlast.
How deep the shadows change has cast!
The blackbirds' group, the crows' harsh caw
Bewail those gone from Waccamaw.

O dreamland South, too short thy stay,
Now yielding to a coming day;

The mart disputes the poet's lay —
But should the Muses all withdraw,
My song will live for Waccamaw.

A TRUST.

EACH trust by God was given,
   Howe'er by man it came;
'T was sealed at first in heaven,
   And bears Jehovah's name.

Inwoven with the matter
   Where human faith abounds,
Beyond earth's din and clatter
   The sacred charge resounds.

'T were better our own treasure
   Should suffer by neglect,
Than, through deceitful measure,
   We forfeit self-respect.

With pledges oft men trifle,
   Their sacred honor sell,
The claims of others stifle
   Through some deluding spell.

When falsely undertaken,
   The duty of a trust
A Nemesis will waken,
   To lay our schemes in dust.

IN MEMORY OF PHILLIPS BROOKS,

LATE BISHOP OF MASSACHUSETTS.

IN stature a King Saul,
　A David in devotion,
An honor to his country, he has rounded life's brief day.
With zeal that fired Paul,
With loving John's emotion,
His sudden loss the thoughtless rouse by God's mysterious
　　way.

His noble form declared
A noble soul's expansion;
The Christ within superior rose to either creed or race.
Affection wide he shared,
From cot to lordly mansion—
The old and young responsive to the sunshine of his face.

A Christian from the heart,
Devoid of ostentation,
In word and deed he pointed to the one atoning plan.
His gifts he deemed no part
Of gold or priestly station—
The man sought not the miter, but the miter sought the man.

A more than bishop died,
'T is not a name has left us;
But one who preached the value of a conscience and a mind.
Upon progression's tide
Moved he who has bereft us —
Such heroes, spurning narrowness, but seldom do we find.

Great Shepherd, God of light,
Destruction's power averting,
Uproot the plant of selfishness, that bane of church and state.
A lordship keep in sight,
Which, Heaven's cause asserting,
Will sound a note 'mid sin's vast wild of true prophetic
weight.

UNCROWNED KINGS.

NOT kingly always he who wears the crown,—
For sceptered craft and impotence insult the state
And foster hate,
While strength of loyalty is broken down.

Before his office self is falsely placed.
His own is first considered — not the people's need;
His wicked greed
Appropriates — all righteous claims effaced.

Of kings not crowned the world may sometimes boast,
Who are but subjects, though possessed of regal power.
They nobly tower,
The choice of Heaven, o'er th' inferior host.

These peerless ones in humblest life abound,
Dynamical within the limit of their sphere,
>> By worth they rear
Authority in despots never found.

They counterpoise the tyrant on his throne
By overcoming influence of honest deeds;
>> They plant the seeds
Of some wild vengeance — to themselves unknown.

The upright statesman is an uncrowned king,
Or he who genius barters not for interest's sake,
>> Who will not break
His pledge to this high gift, whate'er it bring.

And monarch such remains to duty true
When sneer or curse awaits the outcome of his will,
>> When threats to kill
With terror haunt the path he dares pursue.

The best of crowns rewards the beacon soul
Which makes the wealth that earth bestows a bauble seem.
>> Its mystic gleam
Is where the "King of Kings" bears chief control.

THE SOUL OF LOVE.

ADORNED with beauty's choicest grace,
A flower at morning tide,
The future told upon her face
She soon would be a bride.

But, mingled with her budding life,
That made it seem more fair,
You felt a mystic presence rife —
The soul of love was there.

The waves of time had swept along,
Meridian glory fled,
The matin bird had sung her song,
The youthful prime was dead.
Like autumn in its sober vest,
Her looks still debonaire,
The mind, of lasting charms in quest,
The soul of love found there.

'T is evening, and the taper low,—
Companions gone before,—
Long vanished beauty's fitful glow,
She nears the final shore.
Now few and faint the traces cling
Of bloom that years outwear:
Yet — bright as in her time-worn ring
The gem — love's soul is there.

THE STORM SPIRIT.

WEIRD spirit of the storm,
Unpitying dost thou go ;
The proudest and the humblest form
By thee alike brought low.

A panic wide is spread
 Where calmness reigned before;
Thy path of ruin and the dead
 Appals the sea and shore.

Thou addest gloom to night,
 Thy frowning hides the sun;
Retiring shrinks the timid light,
 The herds before thee run.

But why o'erwhelmed with fear
 Beneath thy darkling sway,
When hues divine will soon appear
 And drive the gloom away?

MOONLIGHT AT RIDGEFIELD.

THIS night is like a dream to cheer our
 troubled vale;
Poetic, fresh, above the gross, the stale;
A picture by the hand Divine,
A benison for hearts that pine.

The vagrant clouds are floating on mid air;
They sail athwart the dome serene and fair,—
Arresting surfeit of the eye
Enravished by the moonlit sky.

Thus wandering clouds impend where fortune's gifts
    abound,
That tracing Omnipresence man be found,
That through the shadow we may prize
What surfeit fails to realize.

How lovely yonder silvery orb, the darkened green,
The softened outline and the lakelet sheen!
How sweet the odor of the flower
On zephyr wing from lover's bower!

Alone, fair queen, thou rulest o'er enchanted earth,
Like one to whom an age gives birth;
Beneath thy radiance nature smiles,
Each charm enriched with borrowed wiles.

O hallowed eve so pensive and by angels blest,
Awakening drowsy fancy from her rest —
To fadeless beauties thou dost move,
In words unuttered, fraught with love!

CONJUGALITY.

ALONE I am not if it be
    That thou art 'neath the roof where I may sit;
Thy form I may not see,
    Nor hear thy voice of music and of wit:
Yet not alone am I
Should others be not nigh.

And e'en when many mingle here,
  While echoing halls are filled with merry sounds
That fain the hour would cheer —
Of thee bereft, a sadness deep abounds,
And mocks each friendly wile
That would from self beguile.

Or should the angels take thee hence
  And mar the joyousness that fills my soul,
In prayer, when most intense,
  A nearness felt would every thought control,
More living than the giddy throng
With flattery, jest, and song.

A COMRADE.

WELCOME, friend of bygone years,
  With joy unfeigned I greet thee ;
Life's early garlands dost thou bring,
  Whene'er I chance to meet thee.

Imaged by thy sparkling eye,
  The brooklet dances brightly,
Upon whose margin oft we played
  When shadowing care touched lightly.

Beaming in thy cheerful smile,
  I see the happy faces
Of loved companions passed away,
  With none to fill their places.

Pressing with a cordial grasp
    The hand I freely offer,
I know that one, well tried and true,
    His hand in turn doth proffer.

Time may set its well-known seal,
    Its shears youth fancies sever —
But verdure of thy guileless heart
    Will spring as fresh as ever.

MODERATE AIMS.

UNDULY ask I not
    For this short life;
My dwelling be some favored spot
    With hallowed pleasures rife,
With friendship near, by enmity forgot.

I know that happiness
    From modest springs
O'erflows, while riches fail to bless,
    Except upon the wings
Of charity, alive to all distress.

It is not wealth I crave,
    Where envy stands,
A hideous specter from the grave
    Of peace, with outstretched hands
To ruin by some plot whence naught can save.

Averse to all extremes,
   I find true joy :
It comes not in the wildering dreams
   Of luxuries that health destroy;
Nor poverty nor riches draw its beams.

I know 't is on the tide
   Of calm content,
Where passion's stormy winds subside
   And reason is not rent
By hapless ventures which the fact outride.

Beyond enough for me
   May some one share —
A toiler brave, from envy free,
   With thankful heart for rudest fare,
Whose plaintless want but One alone can see.

"THOSE WE REMEMBER."

ADORNING life's pathway, with pleasure we meet
   Companions who ennui dispel :
The charm of their presence delighted we greet—
   Reluctantly bid them farewell.

But 't is not the contact of hand grasping hand—
   Approval of mind has been reached;
Where friendship is hallowed in mem'ry's choice band,
   Her steadfastness never impeached.

The heart is a witness beyond all appeal
Of forms time will never efface —
'T is this—only this, can enduringly seal
The loved in the past that we trace.

Hence small is the number, unbroken by years,
We prize as when earliest seen —
To whom fond recurrence a monument rears,
Their sod by affection kept green.

They may not be beautiful, valiant, or gay —
Have little the worldly admire;
Like flowers that hide from the glare of the day,
May know not ambition's desire.

Remembered they are for the blessings they shed,
O'ermastering despair through their wiles —
That, ruling the spirit—all selfishness dead,
An Eden have planted with smiles.

DIES IRÆ.

DAY of anger, noted day,
     Earth in ashes melts away,
David and the Sibyl say.

Ah, what trembling will there be
When with searching scrutiny
Every act our Judge will see!

At the trumpet's startling tone —
Which sepulchral gloom shall own —
All must come before the throne.

Death astounded, Nature, too,
Shall be found, as rise to view
Buried forms the Judge to sue.

Hidden things will be revealed
In the record long concealed
When the verdict he will yield.

Dreadful in his lofty seat,
Crime must leave its vain retreat
Righteous punishment to meet.

Wretched me, what shall I say,
To what intercessor pray,
When the just see not their way?

King of awful majesty,
Saving man when true to thee, —
Mercy's font, deliver me!

Jesus, pitiful, recall
How I brought thee through the fall, —
Do not let this hour appal.

Weary waiting, sought thou me,
Interceding on the tree, —
Not in vain thine effort be.

Righteous Judge retributive,
Pardoning grace thy servant give,
Till the reck'ning let me live.

Deeply I a culprit groan,
Face suffused with guilt I moan,—
Send forgiveness from thy throne.

Thou who canceled Mary's sin,
Thou whose ear a thief could win,
Grant me also peace within.

Merit seasons not my prayer,
Yet, good Lord, in mercy spare,
Lest eternal fire I share.

From the goats thy servant keep;
Let me mingle with the sheep,
At thy right their fruits to reap.

When the lost their sins confound,
And the scorching flames surround,
May "well done" to me resound.

Humble, prostrate, I implore —
Contrite in the dust, heart-sore,
Guard me when death hovers o'er.

In that mournful day's surprise,
When, O Judge, from ashes rise
Guilty mortals — hear their cries.

In the mansions of the blest,
Where no storms can reach the breast,
Jesu, grant to all thy rest!

"DEATH IS SWALLOWED UP IN VICTORY."

SLOW beats the pulse in yonder wasted form;
It soon must yield as sweeps the final storm;
No power can save
But His who gave,
While sluggish drags the crimson current warm.

The eager eyes of fond ones look through mist;
Their ears attent for faintest word still list:
But in that room,
Oppressed with gloom,
All signs to cheer the darkness love resist.

An earnest watcher murmurs, "Death is near,"
As faith despondent yields itself to fear;
When lo! a strain
Makes weeping vain—
"Ah, no; not death, but life," with joy they hear.

PARTING HYMN.

GONE, the charm of school-day life,
Gone, the early mental strife ;
   Visions fade from fancy's prime,
   Fact must rule in coming time.
Bravely let us seek the right,
Hopeful scale the rugged height,
   Where, upon her chosen throne,
   Honor waits to claim her own.

CHORUS.

   Bravely let us seek the right,
   Hopeful scale the rugged height,
      Where, upon her chosen throne,
      Honor waits to claim her own.

Promise cheers the toilsome way ;
Born of learning's favored day,
   Clear-eyed Science quick unfolds
   Depths no dreamy age beholds.
Woman's work, so well begun,
Wide and wisely should be done ;
   She may occupy each sphere
   Where her noblest powers appear.

CHORUS.

Principal and teachers true,
School-mates all, adieu, adieu!
    Blessed fruits of Jesus' love
    Be your guerdon from above.
Let us trust, when outward bound,
Crystallized within, be found
    Line and precept fitly given,
    Glowing with the light of heaven.

CHORUS.

HAIL WE ALL THE GLADSOME HOUR.

CHRISTMAS CAROL.

WHY are church-bells gaily sounding?
    Why each pulse with rapture bounding?
Gleams of Christmas shine afar,
Brighter than its Eastern Star.

CHORUS.

    Hail we all the gladsome hour!
    God and angels seal its power.
    Vanquished doubt before it flies—
    Heaven's message fills the skies.

Why are children sweetly singing,
Toward the throne their voices ringing?
Gently folded to his breast,
Children are by Jesus blest.

CHORUS.

Why are strains from humblest dwelling
In the choral outburst swelling?
Of his treasure all partake,
Who was poor for our sake.

Chorus.

Why rejoice the broken-hearted,
Life a blank — its hopes departed?
Christ secured for their relief
Balm to soften every grief.

Chorus.

THE EASTER SONG.

Chorus.

SING loud the Easter song:
   Its story is not long;
'T is spoken in a breath —
The Saviour conquer'd death.

'T is warbled by the bird
Whose springtide voice is heard;
'T is told throughout the vale
By fragrance we inhale;
While every verdant lawn
Reveals it to the dawn.

Chorus.

The brook that laughs and sings,
From fetters freed, now brings
The news that from his side
There came a healing tide;
That 'mid the pastures green
The wave of life is seen.
CHORUS.

The welcome season's birth
That leaves a wintry dearth,
The hopes renewed that glow
Like beams which melt the snow,
Inform us of love's power,
That rules this favor'd hour.
CHORUS.

REASON AND REVELATION.

I KISSED the rod, for Reason said 't were well;
  That murmuring would bring no better fate
Than that evoked by sorrow's present spell:
  The rather I might feel more poignant weight—
The load of conjured grief, which, else unknown,
  Could add no furrow to my saddened brow,—
Which harmless, in the bud and not full blown,
  Would ne'er coerce me from submission's vow.
I kissed the rod, and did not seek to fly:
  For Reason pointed to the Stoic's plan

As best befitting lineage so high
    As that accorded to the humblest man.
I bowed because she coldly said a power
    That placed me on this sphere, by changeless rule,
Would scatter in due season clouds that lower,
    While calling him who questioned her a fool.
But such dissuasion left me in the dark,
While tossed amid the storms of doubt, life's bark.
I could not trace the wildering, distant shore,
Where wearied hope might dwell forever more.
Then as the voyager, spent by long delay,
San Salvador perceived 'mid faith's decay,
From dark forebodings I at last awoke,
When truth upon my longing vision broke:
For Revelation did more clear expound
And cause from dim surmise the heart to bound;
A new compliance set at rest all fear,
And love eternal stayed the rising tear.

OMNIPRESENCE.

HE sees, and only He,
    The secret of life's mystery,—
Its deep unwritten history,—
Each thought the lips refuse to speak,
The purpose strong, with action weak,
The vengefulness, with bearing meek.

He hears, and only He,
The prayer that comes 'mid falling tears,
Corroding needs, appalling fears,—
Where music's soul has long been dulled,
The garden's sweetest flower culled,
The wave of proud ambition lulled.

He knows, and only He,
When time seems flitting cheerily,
How drag its wheels but wearily.
He knows the spirit's strife with sin,
While censure with confusing din
Arises from the world's chagrin.

He guards, and only He,
When storms assert their maddening sway,
As safe as 'mid the gladdening day.
His watch is in the darkest night
The soul can know,— amid its flight,
Till reaching final depth or height.

He loves, and only He,—
The Parent true,— unceasingly,
Like flowing tide increasingly;
By non-requital never turned,—
Repentance smoldering, embers burned,—
His love inborn and never learned.

He saves, and only He,—
Attempt of man erasing not
That subtle and defacing spot.
While traveling the celestial road,
His Son alone removes the load
That keeps us from the pure abode.

I LOVE MY CHURCH.

I LOVE my Church, and not because it is a Church,
But something better than a Church is there.
'T is not the ceremony grand and beautiful
That wins me, but its Lord found everywhere.

I love each Church wherein redemption's plan is told,
The name be what it may, the worship, too.
That Church I know not where concealed the Truth, the
Life,
Nor those its members called who evil won.

Authority is little to a soul athirst;
No broken cisterns can the want supply.
I love my Church because it comforts while I live,
But most because it comforts when I die.

THE BETTER SIDE.

A BETTER side has every man,
And, seeking, we may find it;
Though dross appear when first we scan,
Faith looks for gold behind it.

Companion of the unclean bird,
The dove will lose its whiteness,
And vice when often seen and heard
Will sully virtue's brightness.

A common soul, howe'er defiled,
Illumines,— God creating,—
And sympathy intense and mild
Can lift to heaven by waiting.

Then let us, from the depths of sin
The germ divine unfolding,
With prayer the erring strive to win,
Enraptured Love beholding.

CHILDREN AND THE CHURCH.

MOST tenderly enjoined upon the Church is childhood;
The little ones within Christ's arms
Were shielded from all power that harms,
As safe as birdlings of the wild wood
When mother wings repel alarms.

16

A voice is heard resounding from a lonely manger
   In baby tones and yet divine:
It charges that the Bride entwine
   Her sympathy to ward from danger
The buds upon the mystic vine.

Hence infants to the sacramental threshold taken,—
   Protected by the spotless Dove,—
To God are sealed through rite of love;
   Kind offices in time awaken
A trustfulness that looks above.

When years have sped in which the " line and precept "
     falling
   As daily falls the nursing dew,—
When Duty, Reason brings to view,—
   They openly assume their calling,
And solemnly their vows renew.

The " olive plants " are not our own, but they were loaned us
   To do God's will upon his sphere —
To serve him from the earliest year;
   Such tendrils for our care were sent us:
Then let his Church the children rear.

"HOPE MAKETH NOT ASHAMED."

THE Christian's hope is on the Rock of Ages founded,
  It maketh not ashamed;
Its choice fruition ne'er by matter frail is bounded,
  For life beyond 't was framed.

It strives to reach a heavenly habitation
  'Mid endless streams of love;
Its safeguards grovel not 'mid limits of probation
  Which time and chance may move.

It clothes with courage in the day of persecution,
  Made tortured Stephen calm,
A Paul before Agrippa filled with resolution,
  To martyr's wound a balm.

It cheers when e'en the dearest friend on earth has left us,
  An angel brightening death;
When misery of every idol hath bereft us,
  And naught remains but breath.

O Father, in this fleeting world so drenched with sorrow,
  Where helpless mortals sigh,
Where prospects brightest prove but futile on the morrow—
  May hope on thee rely.

TEACHERS OF IMMORTALITY.

WHAT pleasant tokens teach
Of immortality !
They dwell outside the commonplace;
They breathe in sighing winds,
And chant in murmuring seas;
They haunt us in the moonlight,
Revive in bird or tree ;
Are found within the beautiful
That smiles on nature's face,
Inviting to be dutiful,
To rise from sin's disgrace;
They come in hallowed dreams
That lift from tedious fact,
In forms that bless the past
And in the present act;
They dwell in all the charms of earth,
The remnants of an Eden left,
And he who cannot trace their birth
Of finest sense must be bereft.

THE SILKWORM.

THE silkworm spins around his form,
And from his form the gold cocoon —
To merchandise a valued boon —
Still weaves he on in calm or storm.

His being fades like day in night,
  But not for welfare of his own:
  It fades to deck the richest throne,
Or beauty's charms in halls of light.

He makes his shroud, his coffin makes
  In all this work for others done
  From early dawn to set of sun—
His task completed, death o'ertakes.

And as to silkworm, so to each
  A work is given for day by day;
  Though, not like him, man oft may play,
Yet all must spin some end to reach.

And when we 've wound and wound about
  The thread that from our being springs,
  And man at last his offering brings,
The doom-bell tolls, the lamp goes out.

But as the cheerful butterfly
  The grub unsightly leaves behind,
  Man's clod the soul can never bind:
It quits earth's toil and soars on high.

AT A BANQUET OF THE SONS OF THE REVOLUTION,

ON WASHINGTON'S BIRTHDAY, 1895.

TO-DAY we recall the American man,
  Of elements rarely combined,
A statesman, a hero, one leading the van,
A Christian in heart and in mind.

Like Alfred he lives in a chronicle green,
  Like Winkelried, Vasa, or Tell;
A noble within as in dignified mien,—
His name too a watchword, a spell.

Old England her colonies favored with tea,
  The best that her market supplied,—
With Gunpowder, Hyson, and also Bohea,
Unloosing each tongue far and wide.

But, laden with duties, our ancestors vowed
  China's cup they would nevermore taste:
As Indians disguised to the wharves did they crowd,
The harbor bestrewing with waste.

O'erboiling with wrath, Britain's rulers received
  Report of the act that was done,—
The motherland feeling intensely aggrieved
At treatment so brusque from her son.

At once she determined to flog the rude child,
  As little ones whipped the taxed top;
But soon she discovered, by anger made wild,
  His perverseness the youth failed to drop.

'T was the boy whipped the mother, and not she the boy,
  Rebelling at what he was taught;
Who managed at last e'en her rule to destroy,
  For one somewhat better—he thought.

"Yankee Doodle" was all our militia required
  Their dander to rouse for a fight;
Nor tea nor yet whisky the patriot fired
  Trained red-coats to scatter in flight.

With flint-lock and blunderbuss — ordnance low —
  Redoubt with its cannon they took;
Each man, like old Put., in the midst of the foe,
  A-soldiering on his own hook.

Now choicest of Hyson the dainty may drink—
  The ballot's decision controls;
If impost drive on to a ruinous brink,
  Redress will drive back at the polls.

We brethren in line of such patriot band
  Its purpose should strictly maintain;
Encroachment of party or sect to withstand
  On principle's jealous domain;

Should carefully watch, lest the tyrant invade
　　Those rights won by bullet and steel :
Like shepherds their flocks, in repose of some glade,
　　The wolf in sheep's garb to reveal.

Our function it is that Bartholdi's grand tower,
　　In view of the Battery Park,
Shall shine like the sun, giving Liberty power,
　　Where slavery thrives in the dark.

'T is ours to cleanse if defilement o'erspread,
　　Obscuring our 'scutcheon once fair ;
From sloth's mausoleum to waken the dead —
　　When the ship of state leaks, to repair.

With eyes always open 'mid every-day walk,
　　And love for Columbia's soil,
Our presence a terror, if Anarchy stalk,
　　Its greed for destruction will foil.

To those who from foreign shores kindly apply
　　To relieve us of national sway,
Enlightened self-government, let us reply,
　　Is presumed the American way.

Humanity's chain binds our States into one ;
　　'T is brotherly love best we know.
Verbum sat.　Let the stream of prosperity run,
　　Engulfing misrule in its flow.

Dishonored the man keeping honor from him
Who noblest of governments gave —
Who will not, to-day, pledge his fame to the brim,
Or has not a wreath for his grave.

And shame to the bigot with minimum soul
Who sees but a fraction of earth;
Who welcomes not strangers, from pole unto pole,
That rejoice in our Washington's birth.

And One rules above who the truth will uphold,
And His truth do we seek to defend;
If allegiance to Him in our hearts we enfold,
Our God will He prove to the end.

www.ingramcontent.com/pod-product-compliance
Lightning Source LLC
Chambersburg PA
CBHW020847270326
41928CB00006B/587